How to Research and Write a Thesis in Hospitality and Tourism

A Step-By-Step Guide for College Students

James M. Poynter
Metropolitan State College, Denver

John Wiley & Sons, Inc.
New York • Chichester • Brisbane
Toronto • Singapore

Poynter, James M.
    How to research and write a thesis in hospitality and tourism / by James M. Poynter.
        p.   cm.
        ISBN 0-471-55240-2 (alk. paper)
        1. Hospitality industry—Research.   2.   Tourist trade—Research.
3. Dissertations, Academic.   I.   Title
TX911.5.P69   1993
647.94´072--dc20   92-40805
                                                                    CIP

Printed in the United States of America

10 9 8 7 6 5 4 3

To Michael Poynter
Student, academician, and soon to be researcher

Contents

Chapter Three: Starting Chapter One   43

Chapter Four: The Chapter One Core   57

Chapter Five: Completing Chapter One   73

Chapter Twelve: Writing Chapter Five   **169**

Chapter Thirteen: Post-Study Tasks   **179**

Index   **189**

Preface

This book is the first step-by-step guide to researching and writing an undergraduate hospitality or tourism thesis. Therefore it meets several needs. It is designed to provide hospitality educators with a text for a standard one- or two-semester course devoted to developing and writing a quality thesis. It will also assist graduate students who have not written a thesis in their undergraduate years. Primarily, however, the book is designed to meet the needs of the student who is enrolled in a two- or four-year hospitality/tourism degree program, who must write a comprehensive thesis relating to some area of the hospitality or tourism industry, and who has not previously written a five-chapter thesis or dissertation.

The program described in this book has been under development since the early 1980s. The phrase "how to write" a thesis is not quite accurate, however. This book is not about how to construct sentences, select the most appropriate words, or develop word combinations in the way that best tells a story. In other words, it is not a book about how to write. Rather, it is a book designed to be a companion guide to a student encountering the experience of writing an academic thesis for the first time. In many years of working with such students I have observed that their most common reaction two or three weeks into the semester is frustration. The instructor may lecture about what needs to be done to prepare each chapter of a thesis, but when the student is sitting alone in the library trying to organize information, there is often the temptation to scream "Help!" There are just too many pieces that have to come together all at the same time. In addition, the student new to research often finds that the interrelationships that must be developed between chapters and between components of chapters are difficult to get under control. While the student faces early frustration, the instructor is often equally frustrated. The professor who has advised other thesis writers is very much aware of the many interrelationships that the student must grasp in order to complete a quality thesis. But there is only a limited amount of class time available each week. The student needs to know so many details, especially at the beginning, that it is often difficult to decide what to teach first. To develop a good research question at the outset, the student needs to know everything he or she will learn throughout the term.

This book will fill in the gaps at this early stage. Over several years, I have found that testing students on an early reading of the entire book one or two weeks into the semester gives them the overview they need. It also provides them with a basic understanding of the key relationships. This helps them develop research questions that meet the practical needs of completing a bachelor's degree.

The book is *not* designed to guide experienced researchers in developing sophisticated papers. It is *not* designed to provide all of the guidelines needed for students developing Ph.D. dissertations. [For these students I recommend *Travel, Tourism, and Hospitality Research: A Handbook for Managers and Researchers*, Second edition, edited by J.R. Brent Ritchie and Charles R. Goeldner (John Wiley & Sons, 1993).] This book can be helpful to students undertaking more advanced research, but it is intended primarily for hospitality and tourism undergraduates pursuing an associate or bachelor's degree who are undertaking the writing of a thesis for the first time. Thus this book contains almost nothing on statistics or on research design options. The entire approach of this book relates to the development of a five-chapter thesis based on a student-designed research questionnaire mailed to a narrow target population in the hospitality/tourism industry. Research design and statistical applications have been purposely limited in this book. Most educators who direct the writing of first-time theses at the associate or bachelor's degree level make a conscious effort to avoid requiring highly sophisticated research in order to simplify the process as much as possible while at the same time facilitating the development of an academically sound research project.

Note the order in which the writing of thesis chapters is suggested in this book. The student begins by writing Chapter Two. Next, Chapter One is written, followed by Chapters Three, Four, and Five. There are several reasons for this. First, many students change research questions because their initial library work suggests that their original question either is not "doable" or will not prove sufficiently interesting. Also, in preparing to write Chapter Two you may find some particular focus on which to concentrate. Although this focus may be closely related to the original research question (frequently it is a narrowing of that question), it is often different enough that if you had written Chapter One first, it would have to be rewritten. Because this happens frequently, I find that students tend to accomplish the task more rapidly and more completely when they start with Chapter Two and then go back to Chapter One.

This is a "hands-on," practical approach to writing a thesis. You are given assignments at the end of each chapter. As the assignments are completed over a one- or two-semester term, the pieces of the thesis come together. The schedule of assignments provides a framework based on a standard fifteen-week semester, but it may be modified to meet the needs of individual schools. If you can complete the first three chapters of the thesis during the fall term and mail out your questionnaires during the first week of January, the analysis of data based on responses and the writing of Chapters Four and Five can be accomplished fairly easily during the second semester.

When using this book on your own, first read the whole book through. Then, when approaching each thesis chapter, go back and reread the appropriate chapters in the book. By following this process, you can guide yourself through the writing of a first-time thesis. The same approach will help students for whom this is a required or optional textbook: Read the entire book first, then go back and begin your work. After reading a chapter in the book, complete the exercises at the end. Your thesis will begin to take shape as a solid research project.

This book has benefited from the input of several hospitality and tourism educators. I thank them for their constructive criticism. If you have suggestions or recommendations that will make the next edition better, please write to me at the following address: 6994 East Heritage Place North, Englewood, Colorado 80111. I thank you in advance for your input.

James M. Poynter

Acknowledgments

The development of this book took several years and the contributions of many people. Although I had worked in research both in academia and in industry off and on for 30 years before the publication of this book, the teaching of thesis-writing courses for eight years and the research involved in writing this book taught me more than the actual experience of conducting hospitality industry research ever did. Therefore, I am especially appreciative of those in the Metropolitan State College of Denver's Hospitality, Meeting, and Travel Administrative Program who joined with me each academic year in helping students learn to write a thesis. I would like to thank Claire Thompson, Senior Editor of the Hospitality Division of the Professional, Reference & Trade Group at John Wiley & Sons, for providing me with the opportunity to write this book.

Ray Langbenh, the Department Chair of the HMTA Department at Metropolitan State College of Denver, has been especially helpful. He has reviewed many chapters of this manuscript and has contributed a large number of research examples from the hotel and restaurant segments of the industry. Yvonne Spaulding has also added much through her solid improvement suggestions, her cutting ability to spot proofing problems, and her quality examples of meetings management research. Alma Anguiano, a specialist in Mexican tourism (formerly with the Government of Mexico Tourist Board), Spanish language teacher, and all-around good friend of and to the book, has provided daily encouragement. She has helped make sure that the mechanics of manuscript management have been completed correctly and on time.

Others at John Wiley & Sons and at Publication Services who aided significantly in the development and production of the book and who are thanked for these special efforts include Jane Ward, Editorial Assistant; Beth Austin, Associate Managing Editor; and Mary Bishop, Production Coordinator.

Dr. Robert A. G. Wong, Professor of Tourism Management at the School of Hospitality and Tourism, Georgian College, in Barrie, Ontario, is thanked for helping identify the need for this book as he and I collided in our mutual (and fruitless) search for an appropriate thesis-writing textbook at a Society of Travel and Tourism Educators' meeting in Niagara, New York.

William Heath, Ph.D., Director of National College, is thanked for his continuous encouragement. Bill has been a friend and an inspiration for more than one of my books, but on this one his not-too-subtle suggestions that I get on with it have been especially helpful.

K. S. (Kaye) Chon, Ph.D., with the College of Hotel Administration at the University of Nevada, Las Vegas, is a researcher whose work I have consistently admired. Without his encouragement to develop the manuscript and to write this book, it is doubtful that it ever would have been tackled.

Perhaps those who contributed most to the book, however, are the students who over the years have unfailingly reminded me when I needed to try a different, perhaps less complicated, way of putting a point across (both verbally and in writing), when I needed to extend my knowledge of hospitality research in order to completely answer their increasingly sophisticated questions about research, and when I needed to make some of my own works more research-oriented. Although it is not possible to list all of them, special thanks go to Holly Winber and Cecilly Worgess, whose theses taught me much about what a thesis can be and the doors that a thesis can open.

Manuscript reviewers helped to cut out unnecessary material, hone the material that was left, order the content flow, and tighten the constraints against which the manuscript has consistently strained. I am therefore most grateful to all of the reviewers for their insightful suggestions.

Associates in the Auraria text office and at the Auraria Library contributed substantially by pointing me in the direction of previous research and other publications that helped me either add knowledge that found its way into the book or confirm information that had been planned for and ultimately was included in the book. Especially helpful were Mary Martinez, former Manager of the Auraria Text Office, Dene Clark, Hospitality Librarian, Tom Salas, Graphic Designer, and Kerranne Biley, Auraria Library Computer Search Specialist.

My family has contributed considerably, accepting the fate of those who live with rattling computer keys, manuscript pages all over the house, and reference materials constantly underfoot. Therefore, my special thanks go to my wife, Sorore, and my sons, Lewis, Robert, and Michael.

About the Author

James M. Poynter has worked in the travel industry for nearly 30 years. He has worked in almost every segment of the industry, in 10 countries on four continents. Mr. Poynter received his B.A. and M.A. from the George Washington University in Washington, D.C. He taught with the Florida State University Hotel School, National College, Tallahasee Community College, and Metropolitan State College of Denver, where he currently directs the Travel Administration program in the Hospitality, Meeting, and Travel Administration Department of the School of Professional Studies. Mr. Poynter was the first Director of the Institute of Certified Travel Agents and served as a TransWorld Airlines Educational Consultant to Saudi Arabian Airlines for five years.

Mr. Poynter has conducted seminars for five national travel associations, at 12 universities and colleges, and for a wide range of private institutions. He has owned or co-owned two training and consulting companies and five travel agencies (including one devoted primarily to running tours). Mr. Poynter has been a consultant to a large number of corporate travel departments, tour companies, and travel agencies. He has designed and marketed over 60 tours and personally guided more than 40 tours.

Mr. Poynter was a founding board member of the Rocky Mountain Business Travel Association and the Rocky Mountain Affiliate of the Professional Guides Association of America. He has also served as a Board Member of the Society of Travel and Tourism Educators and the Colorado Authors' League. He is the only honorary member ever selected by the Institute of Certified Travel Agents and by the Rocky Mountain Business Travel Association.

Mr. Poynter is the author of four other travel industry textbooks and more than 60 articles. For two years he wrote a weekly national newspaper travel column. Mr. Poynter was the recipient of "The Education Award" for 1992 (a recognition of "significant contribution to the advancement of education in the business travel community") presented by the Association of Corporate Travel Executives. He has also been selected for inclusion in several *Who's Whos*, most recently the Marquis *Who's Who in the West* and the Marquis *Who's Who in the World*.

CHAPTER ONE

Your Original Thesis

U*pon completion of this chapter, you will be able to:*

1. Identify and list the chapters and the sections in each chapter that constitute the original thesis.

2. Prepare and hand in for a grade a selection of original thesis research questions.

3. Prepare and hand in for a grade a narrowed-down selection of original thesis research questions and justifications for their consideration.

4. Make and hand in for a grade an original thesis style manual selection, including a written justification for your selection.

What Is an Original Thesis?

An original thesis is a major research undertaking, normally conducted at the bachelor's or master's level. It is similar to a doctoral dissertation, though not nearly as rigorous and time-consuming. The original thesis may be your first major research undertaking. It is usually considered a capstone activity, rounding out your overall education and providing you with an awareness of the types of research conducted in the hospitality industry. Although industry research applications tend to be less formal than those required in academia, most of the processes are the same; you should not find it difficult to make the transition. The original thesis is an opportunity for you to explore in depth a specific area of the hospitality industry.

What Is Hospitality Industry Research?

Research is problem solving addressing a problem that is considered to be a felt need. Hospitality research, therefore, is problem solving in which the problem represents a felt need in the hospitality industry.

A more definitive explanation of research is that it is an orderly investigation of a defined problem using scientific methods to gather representative evidence and draw logical, unbiased conclusions. The validity of the conclusions should be demonstrated. In addition, general principles that may be applied with confidence under similar conditions in the future should be developed. Hospitality research is an orderly investigation of a defined hospitality industry problem using appropriate scientific methods.

Each of the major components of the hospitality industry relies upon research found in several segments of the industry. The four major segments are academic institutions, associations within the field, industry businesses, and government.

The Original Research Thesis Chapters

An original research thesis is composed of five chapters. These are titled somewhat differently in various institutions of higher learning; the titles we will use are those that are most often found. The content parameters remain essentially the same.

Contents of Chapter One

Chapter One is titled "The Problem and Its Setting." This chapter sets out the basic framework for the thesis. Its components include: (1) a title page; (2) an introduction; (3) a section relating to the research question; (4) the statement of the problem; (5) subproblems (and usually a discussion of them); (6) hypotheses (sometimes a null hypothesis—see Chapter 4) with discussion; (7) organization; (8) definitions of terms and abbreviations; (9) assumptions; (10) delimitations; (11) a section relating to the importance of the study; and (12) a summary of the chapter. Endnotes (if not included in the text) and a bibliography (unless you use a single bibliography for the entire thesis) follow.

Contents of Chapter Two

The second chapter, often the first chapter to be written, is the "Review of Related Literature." This chapter reviews the literature on the subject being researched. Because of differences in the literature, the titles within this chapter vary with each original thesis. However, this chapter does include some specific elements. These include a title page, an introduction, a section relating to the objectives and purposes of the research, the body of the chapter, conclusions, endnotes, and a bibliography.

Contents of Chapter Three

Chapter Three is variously titled "Methods," "Methodology," or "The Data and the Treatment of the Data." I opt for the third, longer title; it is more descriptive, and the first-time thesis writer tends to identify with it better.

This is the chapter in which you tell the reader (the instructor) the specifics of the research and how it will be conducted. This section will be written before starting the original research effort and will detail each step of the research effort as well as each statistical application to which the compiled data will be subjected.

According to Leedy (1985, p. 108), standard components for Chapter Three include: (1) a title page; (2) an introduction; (3) a section titled "The Data—Primary and Secondary"; (4) a section titled "Criteria for the Admissibility of the Data"; (5) research methodology; (6) validity; (7) reliability; (8) the population (and usually an explanation of why the population being used was selected); (9) the problem; (10) subproblems (usually a minimum of three subproblems are identified and discussed); (11) the data needed (for each subproblem); (12) the location of the data needed (for each subproblem); (13) the means of obtaining the data needed (for each subproblem); (14) the treatment of the data (for each subproblem); (15) item analyses; (16) tables to be formulated; (17) figures to be formulated; (18) graphs to be formulated; (19) charts to be formulated; (20) a conclusion or summary; (21) endnotes (if appropriate); and (22) a bibliography.

Contents of Chapter Four

Chapter Four is written after the original data has been gathered and analyzed. This chapter is usually titled "The Findings." Chapter Four sets out the results of the data in exactly the way Chapter Three indicates that the results will be analyzed. Editorialism is inappropriate in this chapter. It is simply a compilation of the results.

The sections usually found in Chapter Four start with the title page followed by an introduction and several research analyses. The first analysis starts with the research instrument itself and analyzes each item or question listed on the research instrument. Each research instrument item will be discussed separately. Each discussion will start with a restatement of the research instrument question. This will be followed by a section relating to the data needed, the data requested in the research instrument question. Next, attention will be given to the location of the data needed. The means of obtaining the data needed is also addressed. Next comes a statement of the results. A statistical treatment of the data is then provided. At the bachelor's degree level this is normally a percentage or an averaging. These are descriptive statistics. More sophisticated statistical tests or analyses that provide the interpretive value of statistical inference may be utilized, but these are usually found only in theses and dissertations written at the master's or doctorate levels. A table, figure, chart, or graph will normally be included in the analysis section relating to each research instrument question.

After having provided an analysis for each research instrument item, the subproblems are analyzed. Each subproblem analysis starts with a restatement of the research instrument questions relating to that subproblem. Next, a statistical treatment relating to the subproblem data (the group of research instrument questions) is discussed, with the intention of determining more global results. Often this is a statistical comparison of the findings of two or more related research instrument questions. The statistical treatment may be a percentage, an averaging, or some other treatment. Tables, figures, charts, or graphs are usually appropriate as well, and these are provided to back up the more global results calculated in the subproblem analyses.

Next, attention is given to the problem, and problem analyses are considered. The problem analyses start with a restatement of the subproblems and the problem itself. A statement of the results relating to the statistical treatment of subproblem data and, if appropriate, the research instrument items are provided. Where appropriate, statistical treatment of the subproblem results is undertaken, again with the determination of percentages, averaging, or some other result(s) derived from one or more statistical applications. Tables, figures, charts, and graphs are appropriate.

After the detailed analyses of research items, subproblems, and the problem, sections relating to validity and reliability maintenance are provided. Finally, attention is given to the hypotheses, with the author determining whether or not each hypothesis listed in Chapter Three is valid or invalid, based on the findings discussed earlier in the chapter and, sometimes, on statistical applications. Other sections may be included, depending upon the nature of the research. Conclude with a summary of the results, endnotes (if appropriate), and a chapter bibliography (if appropriate).

Contents of Chapter Five

Chapter Five is most frequently titled "Data Interpretation and Recommendations for Further Study." Start with a title page and an introduction. It is in this chapter, and only in this chapter, that you may provide editorial comment. This comment relates to interpretations of the data. The interpretations form the bulk of Chapter Five and must be related directly to the data analyses provided in Chapter Four. Next, conclusions based upon the interpretations are drawn or suggested. Finally, recommendations for further study are provided. A summary completes the chapter.

The Appendixes

To the five chapters are added one or more appendixes. There are usually a large number of appendixes, but this varies from thesis to thesis. Appendix considerations should be discussed with the professor who is guiding your research. Appendix options are discussed in several of the later chapters of this book.

How Your Research Can Help You and the Industry

An original thesis is expected to contribute to the knowledge of the industry. The word original suggests that it is an effort that has not been undertaken in the past. Many students have done research that has contributed to the body of knowledge in the industry. In selecting a research question, the ability to contribute to the industry should be one of your primary concerns.

You can benefit from this effort. Some students have made the contacts needed to land jobs in the industry. Because of the direct benefit to one or more employers that derives from the knowledge developed in their theses, a few students have obtained excellent job offers. In many cases these were offers that would not have come about in any other way.

Other students have found that writing an original thesis has assisted them in obtaining scholarships and grants. For some, the scholarships and grants have come after the thesis was completed and was a way in which the industry recognized their contributions. In some cases, however, one or more companies may sponsor original thesis work through the awarding of grants and scholarships before the thesis is written. These grants and scholarships may be for small amounts that do little more than offset the cost of parts of the thesis research, or they may offer substantial amounts of money and provide a large percentage of the income needed by students to complete their degrees. Students are encouraged to look beyond the immediate goal of completing a degree program and select a thesis topic that will not only be of interest to them, but to industry employers and scholarship award grantors as well.

Holly Winber's efforts reflect a good example of what you can receive as a result of designing a thesis geared toward future industry benefits. Ms. Winber wanted to lead student tours with a major tour company. When writing her original thesis, she selected a topic that related to identifying the most effective marketing tools used by tour companies in soliciting business from students through on-campus travel agencies. She found that there was no central listing of travel agencies on campuses in the United States. She wrote to every accredited four-year institution of higher learning, asking each one if it had a travel agency on campus. After compiling a comprehensive list of campus-based travel agencies, she sent out a questionnaire to the campus travel agency owners and managers asking what tour operator marketing strategies were most effective in marketing tours to college students. After gathering her data, Ms. Winber contacted the major tour operators that offered student tours. She offered to provide them with the only complete list of college-based travel agencies in the country and what she believed to be the only complete survey of effective marketing strategies designed to reach college students. This resulted in Ms. Winber having job offers at the time of graduation with three well-known tour operators. She took a position with the world's largest student tour company.

The Importance of Topic Selection

Dr. David Howell of Niagara University suggests that selecting a topic should be approached with the same caution as selecting a spouse. You live with the consequences for a long time. The thesis is worked and reworked to such an extent that even though you may start out thoroughly excited about your research question, you can become tired of it by the time your original thesis is completed. Perhaps the most important consideration in selecting a topic is to make certain that it is one that you will enjoy working with and will find exciting and stimulating for as long as possible.

Most people find that one of the major problems they encounter is an inability to narrow their topic so that it can be fully treated within a reasonable period of time. Finding a research question that is neither too broad nor too narrow is a challenge few meet well the first time around. You may have to revise your research questions several times. The problem encountered most often is selecting a topic that is too broad, but the reverse problem is also sometimes true.

The breadth of the research topic usually relates to the target audience—those people who will be surveyed or those about whom the study is conducted. This target audience (called the population) must be of a reasonable size; it can be neither too large nor too small. For example, if you undertake the research question "Is there a significant difference between the tasks performed and the roles undertaken by front desk managers?" you have a problem in that there are so many hotels throughout the world that have front desk managers that it would be impossible to survey all of them. Many have more than one front desk manager, in that the title is sometimes used for shift supervisors. Therefore, if you are going to study something relating to front desk managers, you must define the term and limit the number of front desk managers considered. After narrowly defining the terms, a better question would be: "Is there a significant difference between the tasks performed and the roles undertaken by front desk managers working in the state of Utah compared to those working in the state of Georgia?"

Even with this narrowing, there is still a potential for misunderstanding and for the task to be too large. You must consider your ability to contact front desk managers, and determine how to judge whether there is a significant difference between the tasks performed and the roles undertaken. Many will interpret "front desk manager" to mean staff managers working at the front desks of hotels, but does this include motels, resorts, and other types of property? The research question might be improved even more by adding "hotel" before "front desk manager."

This brings us to the consideration of the practicality of a thesis. Most agree that a good thesis question must be researchable or "doable." Another consideration is that key words must be clearly defined. If each reader of the research question has a different idea as to what the question is, the thesis will be in trouble. Ideally, the research question will have few variables. Perhaps the best type of research question is one that has only one area of consideration and no more than one variable. For example, with the research question "Do restaurant manager ethics patterns change with such variables as: (1) years of experience, (2) amount of cooking background, and/or (3) major daily job tasks?" you have to look at a wide number of comparison variables. The need to identify and fully treat each potential variable will be a large and cumbersome task. The research question can be narrowed and defined: "Do downtown Chicago restaurant managers' ethics patterns change with their number of years of experience?" This narrows the number of restaurant managers. It also allows you to look at ethics patterns versus years of experience. With these changes the question becomes doable, whereas the former question would probably be impractical, if it could be completed at all.

Initial Topic Selection

Do your best to make the research question doable and reasonable in terms of both breadth and depth. Consider the target audience (population) and write with precision and clarity. The definitions section will help in clarifying the words you use, but key words need to be as simple as possible.

Review the list of research questions randomly selected from (and in some cases modified substantially from those appearing in) *Dissertation Abstracts*. This list is included with an appropriate exercise at the end of this chapter. Each of these questions was approved by a committee of academicians experienced in identifying good research questions. Do not "adopt" or copy these questions, but review them to gain an understanding of what constitutes a good research question. Keep in mind, however, that even these "approved" questions were often refined even further. As an exercise to help you learn to better state your research question, try refining these questions.

You may wish to test your research question on friends, relatives, and fellow students. Ask them to explain what is meant by the research question after they read it. If several people interpret it in a way different than you expected them to, consider changing the wording.

Initial Population Considerations

The population is the target audience: the group of people that you will ask to respond to your questionnaire. In the research question discussed earlier, this would be front desk managers; in the original version of that question, it would be front desk managers around the world. Clearly, one of the factors to be considered in selecting a population is size: The population that you elect to sample needs to be reasonable in number. It is not very practical to survey all front desk managers throughout the world.

However, as you start narrowing the population base, you start limiting the potential importance of the study. If, for example, the question regarding front desk managers narrowed the population to front desk managers in hotels throughout the United States, the results would not apply to front desk managers in hotels in Europe, Asia, or other parts of the world. Also, you could not justifiably say that the results apply to front desk managers working in motels, resorts, or other types of properties. As you narrow the population, you limit your ability to project from the resulting data.

One of the requirements for an original thesis is that it should be a contribution to the industry. Some narrow this even further by saying that it must be a contribution to the discipline. Be careful not to narrow the population to a base that is so small that no real contribution is made. For example, it would be much easier to survey front desk managers in Miami, but could you project the results to front desk managers in other parts of the United States or the world? Such a projection would probably be questioned. Therefore, it is also probable that your contribution to the industry would be a contribution only to the Miami hotel industry. In selecting a population, you have the problem of selecting a wide enough population that the end result will be a contribution to the industry, but a narrow enough population that the research is practical and can be handled within your mailing and processing budget.

One way of overcoming the problem of studying a very large population is to sample. If there are 60,000 front desk managers throughout the United States, for example, but you have the funds to mail to and survey only 10,000 front desk managers, a scientifically conducted sampling of approximately one out of every six front desk managers throughout the country would provide results that should be similar to the results you would get if you sent the questionnaire to all 60,000. A sampling of one out of six is generally acceptable, but if you went to a sampling of one out of 300, the sample would not be nearly as representative. When identifying a population basis for your thesis, you need to be concerned with the total number of persons in the population base to be sampled, the ability to get an accurate list of those people, the budget that you will be working with in mailing and processing, the sampling techniques that you will use, and the sample ratio (the percentage of those in the total population who are contacted).

You must also be concerned about how well the target audience can be expected to respond. This is difficult for students. Your instructor, however, and others at your college or university, may have supervised the writing of a number of theses. Ask their counsel regarding the response rate of potential target groups. For example, in Denver it has been found that corporate travel managers tend to respond to questionnaires quite well; more than 50 percent respond to thesis questionnaires. On the other hand, it has been found that in-flight services personnel managers tend to respond less frequently; only 20 to 30 percent respond to thesis questionnaires.

The response rate is important. If you send questionnaires to 1,000 corporate travel managers throughout the United States, you can expect to receive more than 500 responses. This is enough on which to base a statistically valid research study. The total population of association member listed corporate travel managers is approximately 1,000, so the expected response rate is a substantial percentage of both the total population base and the total of those surveyed in the base.

On the other hand, there are fewer than 50 in-flight services personnel departments for major air carriers in the United States. If you send questionnaires to all the in-flight services personnel managers and receive a response rate of 30 percent, you will get back approximately 15 responses. This is insufficient to provide a significant contribution to the industry.

The problem is compounded in that each of the major carriers employs a large number of recruiters for in-flight services. The person who responds to a questionnaire regarding in-flight services recruiting may not represent all recruiters for that carrier. In other words, for a study of recruiting at major air carriers, a survey of in-flight services personnel managers would probably not be a good population base.

Reaching all or even a substantial number of in-flight services recruiters would be difficult, however, although at first glance a mailing to recruiters might appear to be a better alternative for this research question than a mailing to airline personnel directors. There are two reasons for this. The first reason is that there is no comprehensive list of major air carrier in-flight services recruiters. The second reason is that there is a rapid turnover rate at this position. Any list that might be compiled would be out of date almost as soon as it is released. Studies have shown that it is difficult to get responses from recruiters because they tend to travel extensively and are often not available. Many in-flight services recruiters have said that they have so much paperwork that they do not have time to complete questionnaires.

In summary, you need to select a population base that is broad enough to ensure a reasonable number of responses, but narrow enough that the responses received will be representative of the total population. To some extent response rate is a function of administrative method. Make certain that a good list is available, and determine whether a sample will be taken or the total population will be surveyed. In either case, make sure that the survey costs are within your budget. Finally, be sure before starting that the expected number of responses will be enough to provide statistically valid results.

The Writing Approach

Develop a plan for writing the thesis. Set aside specific hours each week. Initially, there will be a considerable amount of library research, which means finding a good library and, ideally, a good librarian. It also means making certain that the time set aside to write the thesis includes a substantial number of hours in the library. After the first several weeks, less time will be spent in the library and more time will be spent in writing and correspondence. Most people find that by setting aside a specific block of hours each week for the thesis and doing nothing but the thesis during that block of hours each week is the most effective way of completing the thesis.

The deadlines set by your professor will assist you in moving from one task to the next until the thesis is completed. You may also want to set your own sub-deadlines to meet the deadlines established by your professor. If possible, finish the assignment several days in advance, so that it can be reviewed and perfected prior to handing it in. The review process often makes the difference between a good grade and merely a passing grade.

In the initial stages of research, especially for Chapter Two, keeping notes on note cards and organizing them by the headings within each chapter can be beneficial. Notes are usually kept on either 3" × 5" cards or 5" × 7" cards. The smaller-size cards are easier to transport and to keep up with, but they have less space on which to write; the larger cards have the opposite benefit and drawback.

Once your note cards are organized, you might want to use one of the following techniques to write your first draft: After reviewing the note cards, dictate into a tape recorder, speaking the thoughts that will ultimately wind up in written form. You can speak your thoughts almost as rapidly as the thoughts come to you. For many, this is a good way to get the first, rough initial draft into some type of permanent form, that is, on audio tape. Of course, you must then transcribe the material. However, this is a mechanical task that can usually be accomplished in a relatively short period of time.

A second technique for writing the first draft is to write the draft directly, either in longhand or on a typewriter, word processor, or computer after reviewing the note cards. Some people simply organize the note cards in the manner in which they want their paragraphs to flow and then rewrite the concepts from the note cards in paragraph format. Make sure that all data taken from other sources are properly attributed.

Still another technique is to start from a topic outline based on the note cards, progress to a sentence outline, review the note cards again, develop the sentence outline into paragraphs, and finally, organize the paragraphs into a full draft paper.

Most people find that if they can let their first draft sit for a day or two and then go back to it to refine it, the next draft will be far better in quality. Some find that the second, refined draft is so good that no additional draft is needed. Others will find that they need to write several drafts. Each time you write a draft, set it aside for one or two days so that you can approach it in a fresh manner the next time you work on it.

The Organizational Structure

The organization of the written material is provided by a standard arrangement of sections within each chapter (except Chapter Two, which varies considerably based upon the research topic). The structural framework for each chapter is built around the subheadings or topics detailed above in the section titled "The Original Research Thesis Chapters."

If you set up header cards for the note cards and title them with each of these subheadings, organized by chapter, you need only write the material appropriate for each header card section. For example, under Chapter Three you might have the header card titled "Population." Note cards behind this header card may remind you of the parameters within which the population description must be kept, and an additional card or cards may be utilized to prepare the population description. You may want to use a separate card for each phrase or grouping of words that you want in the "Population" description. These phrase cards can be sorted, and perhaps rewritten, until the right wording is achieved. It should be possible to prepare the section draft immediately after reviewing the sorted and rewritten note cards.

The organizational structure and the writing approach can thus be merged to make the actual construction of the initial draft of each chapter a more mechanical function.

Again, however, remember to follow the steps detailed in the above section on the writing approach.

Selecting a Style Manual

Some institutions have a strict policy about the style manual that is to be followed by all at the institution who write theses or dissertations. If this is the case at your college or university, you need not read this section any further, since the choice of style manual is out of your hands. If, however, your college or university leaves the selection of the style manual up to you, the information provided here will give you some guidelines.

Style manuals provide guidelines as to writing style. A style manual not only tells you how to prepare the standard manuscript page for each normal page in the thesis, but it also tells you how to prepare all special sections such as the title page, endnotes, the bibliography, and appendixes. The style manual will often provide examples of footnotes and bibliographies. It will explain how many lines down on the page each manuscript page should start and how wide the margins should be. It will explain where page numbers should appear and how footnotes should be included: in the body of the text, at the bottom of the page, at the end of the chapter, or at the end of the thesis.

Style manuals differ, sometimes substantially, in their formats. Some people are far more comfortable with one style manual as compared with another one. If the selection of a style manual is left up to you, review all major style manuals and select one with which you are most comfortable. Keep in mind, however, that you must select and follow only one style manual; do not mix the styles of several manuals. For example, educators do not accept following the footnoting style from one manual and the bibliography style from another.

Although there are many style manuals on the market, two tend to be used by almost all writers of original theses. These are: (1) Kate L. Turabian's *A Manual for Writers of Term Papers, Theses, and Dissertations,* and (2) the *Publication Manual of the American Psychological Association* (Figure 1.1). The Turabian style manual is the older of the two, and for that reason it has been utilized far more extensively than the American Psychological Association style manual. However, many find that Turabin's placement of footnotes at the bottom of each page is cumbersome. In addition, many feel that the extensive data required in footnotes is unnecessary when there is a bibliography at the end of the publication as well. On the other hand, many feel that, possibly because it has been used so extensively, the Turabian manual has an answer for almost every question that may come up in the writing of a paper.

The American Psychological Association manual is the most popular manual today, primarily because it includes footnotes within the text of the material, and most agree that it is an easier manual to follow in terms of the actual writing mechanics. Because it is newer, there may be times when you are unable to find answers to questions regarding style, but this is rare.

Review both manuals before selecting one. (There are other style manuals on the market as well. You may want to review and consider using one of these.) You may wish to discuss the pros and cons of each style manual with your instructor and perhaps with students who have already completed their theses. These individuals should be able to give you good recommendations. Remember, however, that mixing styles between manuals is not acceptable. Also, do not take footnoted or bibliography references directly from publications; many books, magazines, and newspapers do not always provide information in the formats required by acceptable style manuals. Some do not provide what is considered in academia to be complete information. Many publishers have their own style manuals, which are usually unique to their own publications and are often not acceptable to many academicians.

Figure 1.1
Reproduced with
permission

To Type, to Word Process, or to Compute

Word processors and computers are expensive. However, many students who will be writing a thesis, especially those who have spoken with students who have already finished the thesis requirement, may rapidly conclude that they must have a word processor or a computer in order to write the thesis. In an increasing number of academic institutions, computer-generated or word-processed documentation is a requirement. However, in most academic institutions it is not a requirement. Theses were typed for many years before word processors and computers became available. There is no question that writing the thesis on a word processor or a computer has definite advantages and can make the job much easier. However, if you have never worked with a computer or a word processor before, you should be hesitant about purchasing one just for the thesis. Many word processors can be learned in a very short period of time if you are already familiar with standard typewriter keyboards; however, many computers, especially many of the less expensive ones, are far more difficult to manipulate, and some require an extensive period of time to become familiar with. You may find it difficult to learn how to use a computer at the same time you are completing your thesis.

Occasionally, an entire chapter is lost because a disk is accidentally erased by a person who is not familiar with computers; this unfortunate circumstance happens to at least one student each semester, according to many academicians who oversee the writing of theses. Therefore, if you use a computer, always make back-up disks and never put more than 10 pages of material on a disk without printing a hard copy (paper) back-up.

Thesis pages must present a professional image. This means that they must be carefully typed (no strikeovers or obvious corrections) or generated by a computer printer. Make certain that the printer attached to the word processor or computer prints the material acceptably well. Some printers do a poor job of printing and a good number of educators who oversee theses reject the printing that comes off very inexpensive, poor-quality printers.

Unless your college or department stipulates otherwise, the decision to type, to use a word processor, or to use a computer is up to you. Review the pros and cons of each approach, but also review the cost. Once a decision has been made, stick with that decision. A change midstream is usually more trouble than it is worth.

Getting Organized—Where and How to Start

To start, collect all materials needed and prepare a draft research question and a list of key words to initiate the library search. In addition, as noted earlier, schedule a period of time each week when you will work on the thesis, and make certain that a solid block of time in the beginning will be library time. If you can obtain a library carrel (a small room reserved in some college and university libraries for those undertaking thesis or dissertation work), check with your librarian and reserve the carrel for the weeks that you expect to be spending time in the library. Draft out a rough outline of Chapter Two. You will probably add and delete from this outline quite substantially as research findings unfold. Armed with your schedule, your draft thesis question, your key words, and your draft outline, set goals to complete sections of Chapter Two, and ultimately all of the first draft of Chapter Two, by the due date scheduled by your professor.

Getting off to a good start will initiate a momentum that, if maintained, will give you the completed thesis by the final due date without undue pressure at any particular point en route.

Summary

An original thesis is a major research project requiring a substantial amount of time and attention. It is usually a capstone learning experience and it incorporates much of what has been learned in other courses. The original thesis consists of the following five chapters: (1) the problem and its setting; (2) a review of related literature; (3) the data and the treatment of the data; (4) the findings; and (5) data interpretations and recommendations for further study. There are specific requirements for each of the chapters, and the contents of all but Chapter Two are detailed in their specifications.

The original thesis should be a contribution to the hospitality industry. However, it can also assist you, the student. Some write on subject areas that are of interest to specific companies and find that the individual companies interested in the thesis constitute good job sources as well as opportunities for funding thesis costs through grants.

The thesis topic selected should be neither too broad nor too narrow in its scope. It must be both practical and doable. Key words should be defined and generally agreed upon. There should be as few variables as possible. To make certain that the research question meets all of these requirements, review it several times and discuss it with other students who have undertaken research before, as well as with the professor who oversees the research.

In considering the population for the study (the target market), make certain that there is a sufficient number of individuals in the total population to constitute a study that will contribute to the industry, but not so many that it reduces the practical potential of being able to complete the research project. You must constantly balance the ability to provide a contribution to the industry with the cost and effort of sending questionnaires to a very large population base. Many resolve this problem through a sampling technique, but the sampling technique must be based on a reasonable ratio. Statistical sampling theory allows inferences about the population to be drawn from the characteristics of the sample.

You should also be concerned about the historical percentage of responses received from the population base adopted. In some cases, it is very good, but in other cases the response rate is very low. If this is the case, you should be concerned about whether you can receive enough completed responses to constitute a valid study.

Plan to spend a considerable amount of time in the library, especially at the beginning of the research stage. Setting sub-deadlines that allow you to complete work prior to the deadline set by the course professor will be beneficial and will give you an opportunity to review initial work and to perfect it.

It is recommended that 3" × 5" cards or 5" × 7" cards be utilized to take notes on data reviewed in the library. From the research notes, you can either tape-record chapter drafts or write or type a draft based upon preparing a topic outline and then a sentence outline from the note cards. Working from the sentence outline, you can then prepare paragraph drafts. The paragraph drafts should be organized and arranged so that they have a logical flow and constitute chapters.

The organizational structure of the thesis is dictated to a considerable extent by the requirements set out for each chapter (except Chapter Two). Again, note cards organized by chapter subtitle can help when preparing original drafts of required sections. Often note cards can be developed into phrase cards, which can be organized in such a way that sentences and ultimately paragraphs can be developed from them.

You will need to select a style manual unless one is preselected by your college or university. Care should be given to the selection of the style manual, and only the manual selected should be used as a reference. Although there are many style manuals on the market, the Turabian and the APA manuals are the most popular.

Once a style manual has been adopted, a decision will need to be made as to how to put the data in final print form. Options include typewriters, word processors, and computers. Typewriters have been utilized for many years, but word processors and computers are becoming popular. Word processors and computers, however, are more expensive, and sometimes they require considerable learning to operate efficiently. The cost and learning time difficulties should be weighed before making a decision.

Organize all materials, obtain a library carrel (if possible), prepare a rough outline of Chapter Two, draft the thesis question, identify question key words, and prepare a draft proposed schedule. By working in accordance with the draft schedule and moving from the rough draft material to the overall chapter draft, it should be possible for the student to steadily and consistently complete each section of the thesis on time within the established deadline constraints.

Bibliography

Leedy, Paul D. *Practical Research Planning and Design*, 3rd ed. New York: Macmillan, 1985.

Discussion Questions

These questions may be discussed by two or more students outside of class, or they may be discussed during class for a more wide-ranging discussion.

1. Why is the thesis often called a "capstone" activity?

2. What is meant by an original thesis?

3. What components constitute the basic framework for Chapter One?

4. What process is followed in writing each of the sections of Chapter Four (what is written first, second, and so forth)?

5. How can your research help you personally? How can it contribute to the industry?

6. What points should you consider in the selection of a topic and a research question?

7. What points should be considered in identifying a target audience or a thesis population?

8. What two approaches are used in writing the first draft of each chapter, especially Chapter Two?

9. What points should be considered in selecting a style manual?

10. What are the pros and cons of typing the thesis, using a word processor for the production of the thesis, or using a computer to prepare the thesis?

Role Play Exercises

Two students may participate in these role play exercises either outside of class or as in-class exercises. One plays the role of the first student and the other plays the role of the second student. Read the scripts and then pick up the conversations in your own words.

1. FIRST STUDENT: It seems like trying to get an understanding of hospitality industry research is very hard. Can you explain to me what it is?

   SECOND STUDENT: Perhaps it is best explained by identifying some of its parameters. One might start by identifying where it is found. But the other part of the question is what is researched.

   FIRST STUDENT: That seems like a good approach. Where is it found? And what is researched?

   SECOND STUDENT: I was afraid you would ask me that. Well, it is found in ...

   ### Continue on Your Own

2. FIRST STUDENT: You told me that academic institutions, associations, industry, business, and government entities conduct research in the hospitality industry. Is there any kind of division of their research and does one of these conduct more research than the others?

   SECOND STUDENT: Whoa! Let's take one question at a time. Yes, there is something of a division of their research work. Academic institutions, for example, conduct ...

   ### Continue on Your Own

3. FIRST STUDENT: I've pretty much decided to buy an IBM computer to use in preparing my thesis. How do you plan to prepare yours?

   SECOND STUDENT: I've looked into it and decided to use a good word processor.

FIRST STUDENT: Have you considered a computer?

SECOND STUDENT: Yes, but I chose to go with a word processor because . . .

Continue on Your Own

1.1. Potential Research Question List

Type your name at the top of the next page. In the blanks provided, type (double-spaced) 10 potential research questions around which you would consider developing your thesis. (Be sure to retain a copy of the completed exercise; you will need it to complete future exercises.)

Remember, your questions should relate to aspects of the industry with which you are strongly concerned. The research question you ultimately select will probably be one of these 10. You will live with your final thesis question for a number of months, so it is best not to select a question with which you will become rapidly bored.

The end result of your research needs to be a contribution to the industry. Make sure that your research question is not a duplication of research that has already been done, and be sure that you can explain (to yourself and others) why having an answer to your research question will be important to practitioners working in your segment of the hospitality industry.

Select potential questions that are doable. Determine whether or not you can obtain a list of members of the population (practitioners) who work in the industry and who can provide answers to your questionnaire, whether or not there is a substantial body of literature relating to the research question, and whether or not those who would be asked to respond to the questionnaire can be expected to respond in sufficient numbers.

To your completed list, attach an Instructor Comment Sheet with your name on it. (Several copies of the Instructor Comment Sheet are located at the back of the book. Photocopy these as needed to complete and hand in the exercises throughout the book.) Place the list and the Instructor Comment Sheet into an 8.5" × 11" manila envelope with a clasp flap with your name typed on the front of the envelope. If your instructor requests it, include a blank, top-quality audiotape (30 minutes long) with your name printed on it, so that your professor may give you feedback.

Potential Research Question List

1. _____

   _____

2. _____

   _____

3. _____

   _____

4. _____

   _____

5. _____

   _____

6. _____

   _____

7. _____

   _____

8. _____

   _____

9. _____

   _____

10. _____

    _____

1.2. Comparison of Potential Research Questions with Previously Researched Questions

Type your name at the top of the next page. In the blanks provided, retype (double-spaced) a revised list of the 10 research questions you developed in the "Potential Research Question List," making any alterations that you feel appropriate after reviewing the list of previously researched questions. As you read the previously researched questions, note how they have been constructed so that they can be practically researched within the short time alloted for completing a thesis. Note also that many of them refer to an identifiable target population.

After reviewing the questions on this list, go back and study your 10 questions. Reword your questions to make them better research questions. When you have completed this task, retype the revised 10 questions in the blanks provided on the next page.

To your completed retyped revised question list, attach an Instructor Comment Sheet. (Several copies of the Instructor Comment Sheet are located at the back of the book. Photocopy these as needed to complete and hand in the exercises throughout the book.) Make sure the Instructor Comment Sheet has the Assignment section filled in and that it has your name on it. Place the list and the Instructor Comment Sheet into an 8.5" × 11" manila envelope with a clasp flap with your name typed on the front of the envelope. If your instructor requests it, include a blank, top-quality audiotape (30 minutes long) with your name printed on it, so that your professor may give you feedback.

Revised Potential Research Question List Based on a Comparison of Previously Researched Hospitality Industry Research Questions

1. _____
   _____

2. _____
   _____

3. _____
   _____

4. _____
   _____

5. _____
   _____

6. _____
   _____

7. _____
   _____

8. _____
   _____

9. _____
   _____

10. _____
    _____

Research Question Examples

From Previous Theses/Dissertations of Hospitality Industry Students

1. Will U.S.-based processing plants with poor records face greater scrutiny if the proposed new USDA food inspection system is adopted?

2. Based on legal cases during the last five years, are there correlations between hotel CEO actions and successful indictments for diverting group revenues?

3. Which of the following factors is of greatest importance to MPI member meeting planners in selecting a site: accessibility, service, or cost?

4. What do hotel CEOs consider to be the best techniques used to control the hotel renovation design costs?

5. Do AHMA (American Hotel and Motel Association) hotel chief executive officers agree on how a unified Europe will affect U.S. hotel companies with properties located in EEC countries?

6. Do America's 100 largest CVBs attract convention business by capitalizing on their "big" events?

7. Do state tourism bureau research directors agree that a longitudinal comparison of world GNP can be verifiably made with U.S. travel payments?

8. What are the perceptions of tour planners working for Canada's 100 largest tour companies regarding tourism's influence on selected economic and social conditions?

9. Do attendees believe that education should be the focus at the Western Restaurant Show?

10. What are the air travel vacation patterns of the elderly German, according to the CEOs of that country's 500 largest travel agencies?

11. What do Georgia's restaurant owners consider to be Georgia's favorite vegetable?

12. What is the impact of direct foreign investment on the ownership position of Jamaican hotels of 150 rooms or more?

13. What are characteristics of the interrelationship between demographics and job satisfaction as reported by hotel managers in seven New England states?

14. In what ways do MPI member corporate meeting managers affect problem-solving behavior in management meetings?

15. What are the top 10 factors that influence the selection and purchase of meeting facilities by national association meeting planners who are members of MPI?

16. Do owners and managers agree on what the optimal span of supervision is in Seattle fast-food restaurants?

17. What need-analysis models have had the highest incidence of implementation for the profit center management concept applied in Pacific border state multi-unit restaurants?

18. Which of 10 selected life-style characteristics and demographic factors do U.S.-based NTA (National Tour Association) member bus tour planners consider most relevant in designing package tours?

1.3. Narrowing and Ranking the Potential Research Questions

Type your name at the top of the next page. In the spaces provided, type (double-spaced) 3 of your original 10 research questions. Select these on the basis of (1) your interest in the question, (2) the practicality of undertaking research on the question, (3) the availability of a target population with which to work, and (4) the "doability" of the thesis. Rank these three potential research questions in the order of your first choice of research question down to your third choice.

Below each question line are several indented lines. On these lines, provide your reasons for the selection of the question. You will need to conduct preliminary research on each of the 10 potential research questions; this will assist you in choosing three questions. Make certain that you explain the results of your preliminary library research relating to the three potential questions.

To this completed three-question hierarchy, attach an Instructor Comment Sheet. (Several copies of the Instructor Comment Sheet are located at the back of the book. Photocopy these as needed to complete and hand in the exercises throughout the book.) Make sure the Instructor Comment Sheet has the Assignment section filled in and that it has your name on it. Place the three-question hierarchy list and the Instructor Comment Sheet into an 8.5" × 11" manila envelope with a clasp flap with your name typed on the front of the envelope. If your instructor requests it, include a blank, top-quality audiotape (30 minutes long) with your name printed on it, so that your professor may give you feedback.

Hierarchical Ranking of the Top Three Potential Research Questions

1. _____
   _____
   _____
   _____
   _____

2. _____
   _____
   _____
   _____
   _____

3. _____
   _____
   _____
   _____
   _____

1.4. Style Manual Selection Form

Type your name at the top of this page. Below this instruction section, type (double-spaced) the title of the style manual you have selected. Give your reasons for the selection of this particular manual. Leave wide margins so that your professor will have an opportunity to make comments.

To this completed form, attach an Instructor Comment Sheet. (Several copies of the Instructor Comment Sheet are located at the back of the book. Photocopy these as needed to complete and hand in the exercises throughout the book.) Make sure the Instructor Comment Sheet has the Assignment section filled in and that it has your name on it. Place this form and the Instructor Comment Sheet into an 8.5" × 11" manila envelope with a clasp flap with your name typed on the front of the envelope. If your instructor requests it, include a blank, top-quality audiotape (30 minutes long) with your name printed on it, so that your professor may give you feedback.

1.5. Preliminary Population Description

Type your name at the top of this page. Below this instruction section, type (double-spaced) a brief description of the population on which your research will be based. You should also include information (at least one paragraph) explaining why you have selected this population. Make sure that your total population base is at least 100. (Ideally, it will be considerably more.) Keep in mind that the study needs to be duplicable. In other words, this must be a population that can be reached with ease by another researcher in case a parallel study or a validation study is conducted. Your professor may give you additional guidelines to consider when selecting a population. Leave wide margins so that your professor can make comments. (Be sure to retain a copy of the completed exercise; you will need it to complete future exercises.)

To this completed form, attach an Instructor Comment Sheet. (Several copies of the Instructor Comment Sheet are located at the back of the book. Photocopy these as needed to complete and hand in the exercises throughout the book.) Make sure the Instructor Comment Sheet has the Assignment section filled in and that it has your name on it. Place this form and the Instructor Comment Sheet into an 8.5" × 11" manila envelope with a clasp flap with your name typed on the front of the envelope. If your instructor requests it, include a blank, top-quality audiotape (30 minutes long) with your name printed on it, so that your professor may give you feedback.

The Starting Point—
Chapter Two

U*pon completion of this chapter, you will be able to:*

1. Identify the reasons why Chapter Two is often the first chapter of the thesis to be written.

2. List at least three important factors regarding the research selected for consideration in a literature review.

3. Complete an internal library computer search.

4. Test refinements of your individual research question.

Introduction

Most people think that you prepare a major writing project by starting with the first chapter and then moving through each chapter in sequence. In fact, various chapters are written based on the logical dependency patterns of one chapter on another. The dependency patterns do not necessarily follow the chronological order in which the completed work is to be presented or published.

In preparing a research paper, many students start with Chapter Two and then write Chapters One, Three, Four, and Five in that order. Many of the appendixes are prepared as the chapters are written, but are normally included last. Introductory pages (such as the title page, table of contents, and tables of graphs and charts) are normally prepared last, but appear first.

Should Chapter Two or Chapter One Be Written First?

There is some disagreement among educators and students regarding whether Chapter Two or Chapter One should be written first. There are pros and cons to both

27

approaches. When you prepare Chapter One first, you feel the logical flow and sequencing of the project and are able to identify some of the parameters of the study. When you undertake the library research to develop Chapter Two, you'll have a good feel for key words and for the constraints within which you'll keep the paper.

The major drawback in starting with Chapter One is that when you undertake library research to develop Chapter Two, you may find that there are far less data available than you expected, or the data may suggest that the research project is not one that you will want or be able to complete. If you decide to change research questions at this point, you'll have to redo Chapters One and Two.

Because of this, many educators feel it's best to start the thesis project with Chapter Two. I agree with this approach and will present Chapter Two before Chapter One. If you are uncomfortable with this sequence, skip this chapter, read the next three chapters (Chapters 3, 4, and 5, which deal with the writing of Chapter One), write (or at least draft) Chapter One, and then return to this chapter.

The Relationship between Key Words, Note Cards, and Outlines

Key words are the data search entries you'll make when undertaking library research to find studies, articles, books, and dissertations related to your research question. You'll work with note cards, library references, and computer searches (internal and external). As you conduct the research, refine your research question as necessary, and prepare footnotes and a bibliography. Title the note cards with three- or four-word headings; keep cards with similar headings together.

Prepare an initial outline of Chapter Two. As your research progresses review and revise the outline as necessary. When your research is completed, you should have a detailed outline, a large number of note cards, footnotes, and a bibliography.

The Initial Research Question and the Literature Review

The initial research question is the starting point for the literature review. The literature review is designed to determine what has been published in the subject area of the research question. Ideally, you will be able to find all major work (and a significant portion of minor work) that has been done in your area of research. Several factors are important. These include: (1) the timeliness of the writing found in the literature; (2) the directness of relationship to the research question, and (3) the validity of the research on which the referenced writing is based. In addition to these three factors, it is important that *all* pertinent research be located. This means identifying all areas of research that might deal with your subject area.

To make certain that your library research is comprehensive, you must consider whether or not there are aspects relating to your research question that will not be identified in a literature review when searching key words. For example, if you plan to use an unusual data-gathering or data-treatment process—and you have determined that this process is accepted in the field—then a discussion of the process, where it has been used, and your reason(s) for using it in the research project should be included in Chapter Two. (But remember: Chapter Two is limited to the literature review. This is not an arena for editorializing.)

Key Words

Look closely at your research question. Identify key words and any synonyms for them. Make a list of key words and phrases, ranking them from most important to least important as they relate to the research question. Keep in mind that the key words you identify may not be used by major reference publications. The Library of Congress book reference, for example, has little or nothing under "travel" and little or nothing under "tour." However, "tourism" lists over 2,000 entries. If you don't find anything under a key word, consider alternate ways it might be listed.

If you find that your key words are not providing you with the number of references you believe exist in the literature, ask a librarian for help in identifying alternate key words. Be aware that the major key words used in one reference publication, such as the Library of Congress listing, may be different from those in other references. Therefore, although you may have identified appropriate key words for one reference publication, you have to go through the same alternate word search when using other reference publications.

Examine the way words are used in the literature. You may be able to add key words or phrases picked up while reviewing the literature.

Library References

The types of library references frequently used in high school work are less acceptable to academicians in higher education. For example, the referencing of information from popular magazines is discouraged. Some academicians discourage use of the material referenced through the *Reader's Guide to Periodical Literature.*

Start by identifying books and subject areas from the Library of Congress listing of published books. Because these are normally available only in libraries, and library access may be inconvenient, some students attempt to locate books from commercial bookstore references instead. The disadvantage here is that commercial bookstores normally reference publications through a three-volume publication titled *Books In Print.* *Books In Print* does not actually list all books in print; it lists books that publishers have paid to have listed in it. These tend to be the books that commercial bookstores would stock. It does not include many research publications, textbooks, and technical monographs. Therefore, for book references, start with the Library of Congress listing; it is the most comprehensive publication of books in print available.

Because it takes so long to produce a book, it may be out of date by the time it is published. More timely information may be found in articles and monographs.

Indexing services will be helpful in locating articles and monographs. Many industry-related indexes are referenced in "internal" library computer systems. Check with your librarian for the names and locations of appropriate industry and industry-related indexes available through your library. Indexes that can benefit hospitality industry students are the *Hotel and Restaurant Index* and business publication indexes. *Dissertation Abstracts* may also be helpful.

Internal and External Computer Searches

Most college and university libraries provide students with an opportunity to undertake much of their initial research effort using computers. Computer searches can be classified into internal and external. An internal computer search is designed to find holdings in the college or university library and in related libraries (usually in the same state or geographical area) from which materials can be received on an interlibrary loan basis. Many college and university libraries will conduct tours of the library and will offer training sessions on how to use the library's computers. Take advantage of these tours and training sessions; they can save you time and aggravation. Some college and university libraries also offer individual assistance to students. Ask your research librarian about these and other services.

External computer searches are designed primarily for those working on their doctorate or master's. However, students undertaking bachelor degree thesis work may also take advantage of external computer searches. These searches tend to be expensive.

They have to be conducted by a trained librarian, and they need to be scheduled, sometimes several weeks in advance. The external computer search is designed to access national research databases, some of which may not be available other than through an external computer search. Many holdings that are not duplicated elsewhere are documented in narrowly distributed computer files, which research librarians are trained to identify and access.

The search is normally billed in one- to ten-second intervals. Because of the expense, research librarians require students to set up appointments in advance. At this time, parameters for the search are identified, especially cost and time parameters. Key words are discussed and various approaches to be used in accessing information are reviewed. This appointment (and the computer search itself) should be scheduled early in the academic term—identifying data and receiving copies of data can be very time consuming.

Many colleges and universities partially underwrite the cost of the external search, which can run into an expense of several hundred dollars. Average searches, however, do not run more than 50 to 70 dollars. If several students are researching similar or closely related topics, computer searches can sometimes be undertaken together, saving costs.

Refining the Research Question

As the research for Chapter Two unfolds and more and more data become available, the research question itself should be revisited from time to time. You should constantly be attempting to make the research question more precise and to establish the specific parameters of the question such that the reader will understand exactly what the study is intended to address. Ask friends and associates to read the research question and explain what they perceive the question to be. Changes should be made until the responses are exactly the same as what the writer intended.

Research may identify areas of the research question that are difficult to prove, or areas where obtaining data is either difficult or impossible. If this happens, alter the research question to make the research more practical. This can sometimes be done by altering the parameters of the question, but more radical changes may be needed.

Reference Cards

When referencing information, several types of reference cards are needed. The first is a reference to the publication; it is often called a publication reference card. This will be used to prepare the bibliography and the footnotes. It is filed alphabetically by the authors last name. It includes the full name of the author as referenced in the publication; the name of the article (if it is from a magazine, monograph, or some other publication that may run articles, rather than from a standard book); the name of the book, magazine, or other publication; the date of publication; the name of the publisher; the International Standard Book Number (ISBN; this number is found on the copyright page at the front of the book); the location (city, state, or country of the publisher); and the volume number and the edition number (if appropriate).

This information provides an easy guide to the publication when looking it up. The shelving location is located in the upper right-hand corner of the library reference card or computer reference. Transfer the location to your publication reference card. When you're ready to locate the publication in the library, the shelving data reference information will tell you where to find it.

Whenever you review a publication, make a notation on the publication reference card indicating that (1) footnote information and data reference cards have been completed, (2) information was reviewed that may be of general value, but specific information for data reference cards was not taken from the publication, or (3) the publication was skimmed and no material of value was found. The reason for these three codings is that (1) data directly quoted or referenced in the body of Chapter Two will need to be footnoted (a referral back to the reference card will be helpful when footnoting), (2) material of a general nature that has been used but not quoted will be referenced in the bibliography, and (3) material that has been skimmed, and has been determined to be of no value will not be referenced, but a notation should be made that it has been looked at (so that you will not forget and go back to it at a later time).

Data reference cards are a second type of student-prepared reference card. These are used for preparing summaries of specific information or quotes that you might use in Chapter Two.

Data reference cards should refer back to specific page numbers and coded references to the publication from which information is being taken. When taking quotes or entering summary information on a reference card, leave room at the top for a headline. This should be three or four words at most and should include key words that will help to file the reference card. Ideally, summaries and quotes will be short and will be able to fit on the front of the reference card. Longer ones, however, can continue on the reverse side of the card, or they can be continued on other cards. All cards relating to the same quote or summary can be stapled together. Reference cards containing summaries of information that may be used in Chapter Two should contain no more than one concept or idea per card and should be titled.

Two specialized types of cards (a good way to organize the cards is to make each type a different color) are prepared for the Chapter One section titled "Terms and Abbreviations." One group of cards will be headed *Terms* and the other will be headed *Abbreviations*. One card will be prepared for each technical term, abbreviation, or acronym with which the thesis reader may be unfamiliar. The definition or explanation is typed on the same card. The reader of your thesis will encounter most new terms and abbreviations while reading Chapter Two. However, the "Terms and Abbreviations" section of your thesis appears in Chapter One. If you prepare "Terms" and "Abbreviations" cards while undertaking the research for Chapter Two, when you prepare to write this section of Chapter One, it will almost write itself.

Some researchers prepare "Importance" cards. These cards help you write the "Importance of the Study" section of Chapter One of the thesis. While undertaking the research for Chapter Two, whenever you encounter a reference to the importance or the potential importance of your topic, research question, or hypotheses, document what was said and where you found the reference. Each card should have reference source data fully documented, and only one reference should appear on each card.

The Continuing Development of Chapter Two

Data reference cards should be kept in a file and organized (using tabs) by related subject areas. When preparing the first draft of Chapter Two, list all the subject areas. Prepare a logical sequence of ideas and concepts that need to be covered in Chapter Two based on a combination of (1) a logical discussion of all pertinent points relating to the research question, and (2) the research card tab headings compiled as the research is gathered and organized on the data reference cards.

Outline Cards and Tab Cards

An outline for Chapter Two should be prepared by noting at the top of blank reference cards (referred to hereafter as *outline cards*) the logical topic headings or divisions into which Chapter Two material should be organized. These include such sections as the introduction, the summary, and other headings, based on what you plan to cover in Chapter Two. Add the tab cards prepared from the student data reference cards.

The Outline for Chapter Two

Outline cards should be placed in logical order, beginning with an introduction and ending with a summary. Based on the outline cards, prepare a first draft topic outline of Chapter Two.

Try not to force data into the chapter. This is one of the more common faults of theses. Many students believe that since they have gone to so much trouble to find data in the literature, virtually everything should be included in Chapter Two. However, some material, although interesting, may not relate directly to the thesis subject. Areas of research that are not directly pertinent should be left out.

Keep in mind that the resulting outline will be a rough draft. After the rough draft topic outline is completed, put all your note cards and references aside for two or three days. Then review the outline and make any changes that seem appropriate. Once the draft topic outline has been completed, prepare a sentence outline. Again, the sentence outline should be put away for a few days and then revisited, making changes that appear to be appropriate.

Remember that Chapter Two does not call for any editorialism. It is intended to be a review of related literature; it is a discussion of the results found in related studies as well as the literature of the field as a whole. It is easy for you to be tempted to editorialize; guard against this at all times. Transition sentences and summary sentences are acceptable. Statements of fact may be made if they are summaries of data. In other words, when information is stated as factual, it should be backed up with statistics or references taken from previously published research.

At this point you should have a topic outline, a sentence outline, and note cards. You should start considering the writing of Chapter Two. Before you begin writing, however, give some thought to what will be footnoted and how it will be footnoted.

The sections of Chapter Two should relate to the tab headings you prepared from the reference cards. Each batch of reference cards located under a tab heading should be pulled and organized into a logical sequence of thoughts, and a draft of the section relating to the concept or thought covered by the reference cards in that tab section should be outlined. Normally, this starts with a topic outline and moves to a sentence outline.

What Is Footnoted?

All data that have been taken directly or indirectly from another source should be identified in footnotes. Concepts also may be footnoted when the concepts came from a referenced publication.

Summary

Many students may initially believe that a book or a thesis is written in sequential order, but most formal writing, including most theses, is written in a somewhat different order. Many start the thesis by writing Chapter Two, the review of related literature. The first step is to develop a research question. From this question key words and key phrases are identified. Note cards are prepared. On these cards reference information is placed. Outlines are developed based on the note cards. As you do the research, you constantly relate the key words to the note cards and to the outline drafts.

The initial research question is the starting point for the literature review. Based on the research question and key words and phrases, an internal (within the campus library) literature review is undertaken. This review identifies books and other publications relating to the research question. However, some reference publications will not reference entries by key words that match those you selected. Therefore, you need to identify similar or closely related words in order to identify all or most pertinent reference publication listings. Keep in mind that you should use the more sophisticated publications. Most students start with the Library of Congress listing of published books, but such publications as *Dissertation Abstracts* and *The Hotel and Restaurant Index* will also be appropriate. In addition, other business publication indexes should be referenced.

Complementing the library index review will be an internal and an external computer search. The internal computer search is a review of those holdings in your campus library (and other closely associated or nearby libraries). You should be able (perhaps with some assistance from a reference librarian) to undertake this internal search on your own. External computer searches are being used by an increasing number of those who undertake thesis research. This is a search of computer indexes and library holdings throughout the United States and Canada. It must be scheduled with a librarian and there is a cost (often subsidized) associated with it.

As more and more data become available through the literature review, you should refine the research question, narrowing the parameters to an increasing degree. Data will be summarized on (and quotes will be transferred to) reference cards. Several types of cards are used, the most common being reference cards. Reference cards are also prepared to identify footnote and bibliography information. These are usually a different color than those used for summarizing data. In addition to these two types of reference cards, tab cards (which identify headings or broad subject areas), outline cards (which organize headings), cards for terms, cards for abbreviations, and importance cards are often prepared to assist in the development of Chapter Two and for the preparation of appropriate sections of Chapter One. By reviewing tab and outline cards, an initial outline of Chapter Two is prepared. You should be careful not to include data that are not pertinent to your thesis.

From the outline, a draft of Chapter Two is written. Footnotes are referenced, based on the reference cards from which the data in the rough draft are taken. Keep in mind that all facts and data need to be footnoted and referenced; Chapter Two contains no editorialism. All facts and data presented need to be referenced.

Discussion Questions

These questions may be discussed outside of class, or they may be discussed during class for a more wide-ranging discussion.

1. The writing of various chapters in a major formal writing project is usually undertaken in a time sequence based on what type of pattern?

2. What is the major drawback in starting the writing of a thesis with Chapter One?

3. Reference note cards should be titled with headings consisting of approximately how many words?

4. What is the starting point for the literature review?

5. What three factors are important in selecting material to be included in the literature review?

6. Where should all facts and data that have been taken directly or indirectly from another source be identified in the thesis?

7. When considering key words, why should you consider alternate ways a word might be listed in a specific reference?

8. Why should you avoid editorialism in Chapter Two?

9. Does *Books in Print* actually list all books that are currently in print? Explain your answer.

10. Why do most libraries charge for completing external computer searches?

Role Play Exercises

Two students may participate in these role play exercises either outside of class or as in-class exercises. One plays the role of the first student and the other plays the role of the second student. Read the scripts and then pick up the conversations in your own words.

1. **FIRST STUDENT:** It seems like there are a lot of different cards I need to get and fill out if I'm going to be able to write Chapter Two. I'm confused. What are the names of these different kinds of cards?

   SECOND STUDENT: One is a type of status card. Another type is a data reference card. Some of these are for quotes and some are for summaries. Those that are used for summaries are called summary information cards. There are also tab reference cards. These have a small tab at the top. Outline cards are another type of card. And you will probably want to maintain cards on which to record terms, abbreviations, and references to reasons why your study is considered important, even though these relate more to the writing of Chapter One of your thesis.

   FIRST STUDENT: That is a lot of different kinds of cards. What purposes do they all serve?

   SECOND STUDENT: Let's take them one by one and I will identify the purpose of each. The first type of card is...

   ### Continue on Your Own

2. **FIRST STUDENT:** I understand that some people start their theses by writing Chapter One and then writing Chapter Two and continuing to write one chapter after the other in the same order in which they appear in the thesis after it is finally finished. This thesis book, however, suggests starting with Chapter Two. I guess there is some reason for that. What are the advantages and disadvantages of starting the thesis with Chapter Two?

   SECOND STUDENT: As you suggest, there are both advantages and disadvantages. Let me review the advantages first. Perhaps the most advantageous reason for starting with Chapter Two is...

   ### Continue on Your Own

3. **FIRST STUDENT:** I have read that there is a close relationship between the initial research question and the literature review. I suppose there should be some type of a relationship, but why should it be a close one?

   SECOND STUDENT: It's really a matter of dependency. The entire literature review depends on the research question. Let me explain why and how this works. First...

   ### Continue on Your Own

2.1. Preliminary Research Question

Type your name at the top of this page. Below this instruction section, type (double-spaced) your research question. Remember, it should be a question rather than a statement. It needs to be practical, that is, within limited constraints. Ideally, some indication of the population will be included in the research question. When writing your research question, leave wide margins on both sides of the paper so that comments may be made by the instructor. Remember, your research question should be only one question and should end with a question mark. (Be sure to retain a copy of the completed exercise; you will need it to complete future exercises.)

To this completed form attach an Instructor Comment Sheet. (Several copies of the Instructor Comment Sheet are located at the back of the book. Photocopy these as needed to complete and hand in the exercises throughout the book.) Make sure the Instructor Comment Sheet has the Assignment section filled in and that it has your name on it. Place this form and the Instructor Comment Sheet into an 8.5" × 11" manila envelope with a clasp flap with your name typed on the front of the envelope. If your instructor requests it, include a blank, top-quality audiotape (30 minutes long) with your name printed on it, so that your professor may give you feedback.

2.2. The Development of an External Computer Search Estimate

Type your name at the top of the next page. In the blanks provided, type the information called for in developing an estimate of an external computer search to be prepared in a search meeting or in a series of search meetings between you and your research librarian.

To develop the estimate, set up an appointment with the research librarian who conducts computer searches. Make sure the librarian understands that the purpose of your meeting is to develop an estimate for the search and not to conduct the search. Before meeting with the research librarian, complete the first exercise in this chapter, and be sure to bring a copy of your ten key words and phrases with you to the meeting (see Exercise 2.3). Also bring a typed copy of your research question. This information will help the research librarian identify databases that will be appropriate to access in detail. Complete the external computer search estimate during your meeting with the research librarian, and ask the research librarian to sign the estimate.

To your completed external computer search estimate, attach an Instructor Comment Sheet. (Several copies of the Instructor Comment Sheet are located at the back of the book. Photocopy these as needed to complete and hand in the exercises throughout the book.) Make sure the Instructor Comment Sheet has the Assignment section filled in and that it has your name on it. Place the external computer search estimate and the Instructor Comment Sheet into an 8.5" × 11" manila envelope with a clasp flap with your name typed on the front of the envelope. If your instructor requests it, include a blank, top-quality audiotape (30 minutes long) with your name printed on it, so that your professor may give you feedback.

External Computer Search Estimate

Research Question for which the search will be conducted: _____

_____

Name of librarian preparing the estimate (please print): _____

_____

Name of librarian who will complete the search (if different): _____

_____

List of key words or phrases to be cross-referenced:

1. _____   4. _____

2. _____   5. _____

3. _____   6. _____

List the database(s) you and the research librarian plan to access (rank them from most to least promising). Note the estimated time, the rate, and the estimated total cost of accessing each database.

Database Title	Time	Rate	Total Cost
1.			
2.			
3.			
4.			
5.			

If this computer search will be subsidized, explain the subsidy or expected subsidy.

_____

_____

Estimated total cost of this search: $_____

Signature of librarian preparing estimate: _____

2.3. The Selection of Key Words and Key Phrases

Type your name at the top of the next page. In the blanks provided, type a list of the ten key words or key phrases that you believe to be of greatest benefit in researching the literature for the writing of Chapter Two.

To assist you in identifying key words and phrases, review your research question, and pull from it nouns, pronouns, and two- or three-word phrases that encompass some key or important part of the question. You may want to photocopy the next page and prepare your initial selection in draft format (in pencil or typed onto a photocopy). Let this sit for a day or two, and go back to it after giving some thought to the key words and phrases you selected. You may want to complete the next exercise (number four) and then revise this exercise. Your discussion with the research librarian may result in your selecting more appropriate key words or phrases.

To your completed list of key words and phrases, attach an Instructor Comment Sheet. (Several copies of the Instructor Comment Sheet are located at the back of the book. Photocopy these as needed to complete and hand in the exercises throughout the book.) Make sure the Instructor Comment Sheet has the Assignment section filled in and that it has your name on it. Place the list and the Instructor Comment Sheet into an 8.5" × 11" manila envelope with a clasp flap with your name typed on the front of the envelope. If your instructor requests it, include a blank, top-quality audiotape (30 minutes long) with your name printed on it, so that your professor may give you feedback.

List of Key Words and Key Phrases

1. _____

2. _____

3. _____

4. _____

5. _____

6. _____

7. _____

8. _____

9. _____

10. _____

2.4. Chapter Two First Draft

Prepare an initial draft of Chapter Two (the review of related literature). The manuscript should be typed (or printed out), double-spaced, with the pages numbered and stapled or bound together. Print your name in the top right corner of each page. (Be sure to retain a copy of the completed exercise; you will need it to complete future exercises.)

This initial draft of Chapter Two should be no fewer than five pages in length and should contain a minimum of ten footnotes. A minimum of four different publications should be shown in the bibliography. Remember that there should be no editorialism in this or in any future draft of Chapter Two.

To your completed first draft of Chapter Two, attach an Instructor Comment Sheet. (Several copies of the Instructor Comment Sheet are located at the back of the book. Photocopy these as needed to complete and hand in the exercises throughout the book.) Make sure the Instructor Comment Sheet has the Assignment section filled in and that it has your name on it. Place the first draft of Chapter Two and the Instructor Comment Sheet into an 8.5" × 11" manila envelope with a clasp flap with your name typed on the front of the envelope. If your instructor requests it, include a blank, top-quality audiotape (30 minutes long) with your name printed on it, so that your professor may give you feedback.

CHAPTER THREE

Starting Chapter One

*U*pon completion of this chapter, you will be able to:

1. List the front "mechanical" pages that precede the introduction to Chapter One.

2. Explain why tables of contents, charts, graphs, and figures can only be speculative drafts at this stage in their preparation.

3. Prepare an inside title page for your thesis.

4. Draft an introduction to Chapter One.

Introduction

As the work on Chapter Two progresses, the development of Chapter One can be undertaken. The writing of the front pages will be somewhat mechanical. Many people like to start Chapter One by preparing these pages to get the formal structure of the paper underway and produce some "end product."

The next section that is usually drafted is the introduction to Chapter One. This is another section that many people find easy to develop early. The introduction to Chapter One will probably be rewritten one or more times, based on the final content of Chapter One.

In this chapter, the only parts of Chapter One to be addressed will be the front pages and the introduction. However, the concept of the population will be revisited with the idea of honing the description. In addition, a general problem found in the writing of Chapter One (and most other chapters) will be discussed: the problem of saying what you mean and meaning what you say.

The Mechanics of Front Pages

Several pages precede Chapter One. These include: (1) the outside title page; (2) the inside title page; (3) the table of contents; (4) tables of charts, graphs, tables, and figures;

and (5) a title page for Chapter One. The first four of these preliminary pages are usually finalized after Chapter Five and the Appendixes have been completed. They are often the last documents to be prepared before the thesis is handed in. However, many colleges and universities encourage students to consider these pages early in the preparation of the thesis. Therefore, some professors will expect draft copies of these pages to be prepared and handed in with Chapter One. Nevertheless, all recognize that the table of contents and the tables of charts, graphs, tables, and figures are speculative at this stage. The development of drafts is required primarily to help you understand what will be needed, and to help you start thinking in terms of the charts, graphs, tables, and figures that will be prepared.

The cover page (also called the outside title page) is a logical starting point and the most visual page of the thesis. It shows the title of the thesis in bold capital letters centered on the top third or half of the page. Most colleges and universities expect you to have your name on this page, usually in smaller type, centered. Many institutions require the cover page to include the emblem of the department or the college (Figure 3.1 shows a sample title page). Since title page requirements vary from institution to institution (sometimes from department to department), check with your professor to determine your institution's requirements.

The inside title page also shows the title of the thesis in bold capital letters, but the type is not as large. Your name, the course number, and the year are usually shown (see Figure 3.2 for an example of an inside cover page). Check with your professor to determine any requirements that may vary from those listed here.

The table of contents is straightforward. It does not list the outside and inside cover pages. It starts with the table of contents and lists all pages that preceded Chapter One, in lower-case Roman numerals. Each chapter is listed (many professors require you to list the sections of each chapter as well), identified by its appropriate page number in Arabic numerals. Most professors expect footnotes (if your style manual calls for them to be listed at the end of each chapter) and bibliographies to be listed separately. Most also expect each appendix to be listed and identified by title rather than number. At this stage, only a draft can be prepared; page numbers are left out. Some professors expect the table of contents to be revised as each section of the paper is completed. (See Figure 3.3 for an example of a table of contents.) Check with your professor to determine any requirements that may vary from those listed here.

Usually, the tables of charts, graphs, tables, and figures are separate tables. Many professors expect a draft of these tables to be prepared along with Chapter One, even though most charts, graphs, tables, and figures will appear in Chapters Three, Four, and Five. This will be a rough draft that will change substantially as the thesis is developed. Preparing a rough draft will encourage you to start thinking about the charts, graphs, tables, and figures that you will use. (See Figure 3.4 for an example of a table of charts, Figure 3.5 for an example of a table of graphs, Figure 3.6 for an example of a table of tables, and Figure 3.7 for an example of a table of figures.) Check with your professor to determine any requirements that may vary from those listed here.

The title page for Chapter One uses the same format as the other chapter title pages. Centered approximately one-fourth down the page are the words CHAPTER ONE in capital letters. Between halfway and two-thirds down the page is the title of chapter one, THE PROBLEM AND ITS SETTING, in capital letters. Centered near the bottom of the page is the page number. Figure 3.8 is an example of a Chapter One title page. As with other parts of the thesis, be sure to comply with departmental or institutional requirements when preparing your chapter one title page.

A STUDY OF RESTAURANT WINE LISTS IN MIAMI

by T.K. Samisan

The

HOSPITALITY (HOTEL/RESTAURANT), MEETING AND TRAVEL ADMINISTRATION DEPARTMENT

of

METROPOLITAN STATE COLLEGE

DENVER, COLORADO USA

Figure 3.1
*Modified Thesis
Component. Re-
produced with
permission.*

A STUDY TO IDENTIFY THE COMMON OBJECTIVES
IN TRAINING PROGRAMS FOR NEW TOURISM INTERNS
IN SELECTED STATE AND NATIONAL PARKS

by

Betty Fielding

HMT 404

May 1991

Presented to the
Hospitality, Meeting, and Travel Department
Metropolitan State College
Denver, Colorado

Figure 3.2
*Modified MSCD
HMTA Thesis
Component. Re-
produced with
permission.*

TABLE OF CONTENTS

Figure 3.3
Modified MSCD HMTA Thesis Component. Reproduced with permission.

TABLE OF CHARTS

Figure 3.4
Modifed MSCD HMTA Thesis Component. Reproduced with permission.

TABLE OF GRAPHS

Figure 3.5
Modifed MSCD HMTA Thesis Component. Reproduced with permission.

TABLE OF TABLES

Figure 3.6
Modifed MSCD HMTA Thesis Component. Reproduced with permission.

TABLE OF FIGURES

Figure 3.7
Modifed MSCD HMTA Thesis Component. Reproduced with permission.

/   CHAPTER ONE

THE PROBLEM AND ITS SETTING

Figure 3.8
*Modifed MSCD
HMTA Thesis
Component. Re-
produced with
permission.*

ix

Writing the Chapter One Introduction

You may have heard the old saying that when writing or speaking you should "Tell them what you're going to say, tell them, and tell them what you said." The introduction and the conclusion form an enclosure around the body of Chapter One. The introduction "tells them what you're going to say." The introduction tells the reader what is in the chapter. For an understanding of how this works, glance at the introduction to this chapter; notice how the introduction briefly and concisely tells the reader what the chapter is about. Some people try to set arbitrary guidelines on the length of the introduction, but it depends on the content and length of the chapter itself. There are no hard and fast rules regulating the introduction's length.

The introduction to Chapter One does double duty. In addition to telling the reader what Chapter One is going to cover, it tells the reader what the thesis is all about. As a result, the introduction to Chapter One may be longer than the introductions to the other chapters.

Start by writing the second part of your introduction first. This is the introduction to Chapter One. One of the best ways to prepare the introduction is to go to each of the interior headings of Chapter One, that is, each of the sections and subsections. Write one sentence for each section. (Some of the longer sections may take two or three sentences.) Organize the sentences into a logical structure until you have a smoothly flowing, concise discussion of Chapter One. This is the second part of the Chapter One introduction.

After completing the introduction to Chapter One, go back to the first part of the introduction, which is an overview of the thesis itself, usually no longer than one or two paragraphs. To prepare this overview, read the summary sections of each chapter in this book that relate to Chapters One through Five of the typical thesis, give some thought as to how each summary relates to your thesis, and write one or two sentences about how your thesis relates. Again, group these sentences into a logical flow.

You may find it difficult to write the first draft of the introduction at this point, because Chapter One has not yet been written. Some people prefer to write the first draft of the introduction after the body of the chapter has been written. However, if you rough out the introduction first, you should be able to go back to it after you complete Chapter One and make any necessary changes without much difficulty. Both approaches work.

The Population Revisited

This an excellent opportunity to revisit the population of the research paper. Chapter Three calls for a formal discussion of the population. However, it is during the consideration of Chapter One that you must decide what population will be surveyed. As pointed out in the initial discussion of the research population (see Chapter 1 of this book), you must identify a population that is large enough to provide a sufficient number of responses, yet narrowly enough defined to have significantly similar interests. It is also important to identify some way of either reaching all the population or sampling the population. Some professors require that 100, 200, 300, or more questionnaires be mailed (the suggested minimum in this textbook is 100) so that 50, 100, or more responses can be expected to be received. If this is the case, obviously a population of at least the size required by the professor will be needed.

Since undertaking the initial consideration of your population, you should have attempted to narrow the population to a manageable size, and you should have identified a population source. You should also consider whether or not the list and the mailing costs will be more than you can afford. If it is, you should seriously consider adopting a different research topic. Remember that without careful attention to the population, the research results will probably be less than satisfactory.

Say What You Mean and Mean What You Say

One of the major problems students encounter when writing is the tendency to not evaluate what is written. Each word must be selected for preciseness of meaning. After writing a section, go back and ask two questions after each sentence: (1) Is this exactly what I meant? (2) Is this clear to the reader?

Don't exaggerate findings beyond a reasonable population. For example, if you read a study that says 76 percent of all wait staff working in 100 selected restaurants in the St. Louis area are female, don't jump to the conclusion that the wait staff at all restaurants throughout the country are predominently female. This may well be the case, but a sampling of 100 restaurants in St. Louis is insufficient data on which to base such a generalization.

Summary

The work on Chapter One normally starts with the "mechanical" pages found at the beginning. These include the outside title page of the thesis, the inside title page, the table of contents, tables of charts, graphs, tables, and figures, and a title page for Chapter One. In addition, the introduction to the first chapter precedes the writing of the body and the conclusion. Many of these introductory pages cannot be finished until the thesis is concluded, but initial drafts of them can be prepared at an early stage in the writing of the thesis. By preparing early drafts, you have a foundation on which you can build a strong thesis. If you prepare draft introductory pages in the beginning and revise them periodically, when the thesis is done you can finish up the introductory pages by doing a relatively easy revision.

This chapter contains samples of the introductory pages that appear before the introduction to Chapter One. In the exercises that follow, you will be asked to prepare similar documents for the thesis you are writing. Remember, these are only initial drafts.

The introduction to Chapter One serves as an introduction to the entire thesis as well. The first part of the introduction consists of one or two paragraphs that summarize each chapter of the thesis. The last part introduces Chapter One. It summarizes each section of the chapter.

The introduction to Chapter One is a rough draft at this stage. Be prepared to go back and revise it as work on the thesis continues.

The research population was considered in Chapter 1 of this book; it is expected that you have researched potential population sources and have identified a population appropriate to your thesis. You will be expected to identify the exact population and provide parameters defining it.

A final point considered in this chapter is a problem frequently encountered by students new to writing: the problem of saying what you mean and meaning what you say. Go over all your material and ask yourself if what is said is what is really meant and if what is really meant is actually what is said.

Discussion Questions

These questions may be discussed by two or more students outside of class, or they may be discussed during class for a more wide-ranging discussion.

1. After the front "mechanical" pages, which section is drafted next?

2. What two questions should you ask after going back over a section of the thesis that has been drafted?

3. What pages precede the start of Chapter One?

4. If the list of the proposed population for the thesis study is more expensive than you can afford, what should you consider doing?

5. What page presents a logical starting point and is the most visual page of the thesis?

6. A formal discussion of the population appears in Chapter Three of the research paper, so why is the population considered when writing Chapter One?

7. What appears on the inside title page of the thesis?

8. The introduction to Chapter One consists of two distinct parts. What are they?

9. The page numbers of what pages appearing in the table of contents are shown in lower-case Roman numerals?

10. What appears on the title page for Chapter One?

Role Play Exercises

Two students may participate in these role play exercises either outside of class or as in-class exercises. One plays the role of the first student and the other plays the role of the second student. Read the scripts and then pick up the conversations in your own words.

1. FIRST STUDENT: There seem to be a lot of pages in the thesis that come before the first chapter. Many of these are pages or sections that really can't be completed until all the thesis chapters are finished. Why should they even be considered until then?

    SECOND STUDENT: It does seem logical that sections of the thesis such as the table of contents and the tables of charts, graphs, tables, and figures should not be prepared until after the thesis chapters have been completed. However...

    Continue on Your Own

2. FIRST STUDENT: It seems like a lot of work having to write the introduction to the thesis itself as a part of the introduction to Chapter One. This means that I have to read a lot of this textbook that I would otherwise logically not read until later in the term. It also means that I have to give a lot of thought to the various parts of my thesis that I would prefer to not have to think about until later. Why shouldn't I be allowed to just leave this section altogether, write an introduction to Chapter One after I finish the body to Chapter One, and write the section that is the introduction to the thesis after the whole thesis has been finished? It seems like it would be a lot easier to do it that way.

    SECOND STUDENT: It might be easier. However...
    Continue on Your Own

3. FIRST STUDENT: The phrase "say what you mean and mean what you say" is sort of catchy, but I really don't know what it means.

    SECOND STUDENT: You're right. It is catchy. It is also important. Let me explain what it means and why it is important. Essentially it means that...
    Continue on Your Own

3.1. The Preparation of First Drafts of Pre-Chapter One Pages and The Chapter One Title Page

Review the information in this chapter regarding preliminary pages for the thesis and the examples of preliminary pages that have been provided. In addition, review the information relating to the preparation of the title pages and the examples of those pages. (Be sure to retain a copy of the completed exercise; you will need it to complete future exercises.)

Prepare a first draft of the following preliminary pages for your thesis: outside title page, inside title page, table of contents, table of charts, table of graphs, table of tables, and table of figures. In addition, prepare a first draft of the title page for the first chapter of your thesis. Be sure to type your name at the top of each of these draft pages.

To your completed first draft pages and Chapter One title page, attach an Instructor Comment Sheet. (Several copies of the Instructor Comment Sheet are located at the back of the book. Photocopy these as needed to complete and hand in the exercises throughout the book.) Make sure the Instructor Comment Sheet has the Assignment section filled in and that it has your name on it. Place the draft pages, the Chapter One title page draft, and the Instructor Comment Sheet into an 8.5" × 11" manila envelope with a clasp flap with your name typed on the front of the envelope. If your instructor requests it, include a blank, top-quality audiotape (30 minutes long) with your name printed on it, so that your professor may give you feedback.

3.2. First Draft of the Introduction to Chapter One

Review the information in this chapter about writing the introduction to Chapter One. Be sure to note that this is also an introduction to the entire thesis. Prepare a first draft of the introduction to Chapter One of your thesis. This initial draft may be much longer than the final introduction, but try to keep it to three pages or less, double-spaced. Type your name at the top of each page of your draft. (Be sure to retain a copy of the completed exercise; you will need it to complete future exercises.)

To your completed first draft of the introduction to Chapter One, attach an Instructor Comment Sheet. (Several copies of the Instructor Comment Sheet are located at the back of the book. Photocopy these as needed to complete and hand in the exercises throughout the book.) Make sure the Instructor Comment Sheet has the Assignment section filled in and that it has your name on it. Place the draft introduction to Chapter One and the Instructor Comment Sheet into an 8.5" × 11" manila envelope with a clasp flap with your name typed on the envelope. If your instructor requests it, include a blank, top-quality audiotape (30 minutes long) with your name printed on it, so that your professor may give you feedback.

3.3. Second Draft of Thesis Population

Review the following: (1) information in this chapter regarding the population; (2) your first draft of the population section of your thesis; and (3) your instructor's comments regarding your first draft of the population section. Based on these, prepare a second draft of the population section. Type your name at the top of each page of this second draft.

To your completed second draft of the population section of your thesis, attach an Instructor Comment Sheet. (Several copies of the Instructor Comment Sheet are located at the back of the book. Photocopy these as needed to complete and hand in the exercises throughout the book.) Make sure the Instructor Comment Sheet has the Assignment section filled in and that it has your name on it. Place the second draft of the population and the Instructor Comment Sheet into an 8.5" × 11" manila envelope with a clasp flap with your name typed on the envelope. If your instructor requests it, include a blank, top-quality audiotape (30 minutes long) with your name printed on it, so that your professor may give you feedback.

CHAPTER FOUR

The Chapter One Core

U*pon completion of this chapter, you will be able to:*

1. Write an initial draft statement of the problem, and from that statement write three subproblems.

2. Sequence the components of Chapter One, from the research question down to delimitations.

3. Explain why the research question is considered the most important element of Chapter One.

4. Describe the ingredients of the "Organization of the Paper" section of Chapter One and discuss what should be avoided and what should be included in the "Organization of the Paper" section.

Introduction

The core of Chapter One is made up of the following sections: (1) the research question; (2) a statement of the problem; (3) subproblems; (4) hypotheses; (5) a short paragraph regarding the organization of the paper; (6) a section relating to the definition of terms and abbreviations; (7) assumptions; (8) delimitations; and (9) one or more paragraphs regarding the importance of the study. An introduction and a summary form the outside barriers that encompass the core of Chapter One.

This chapter will discuss the importance of each of the Chapter One core sections and the process of refining the research question into its final form. The statement of the problem will also be addressed. This chapter will identify how subproblems are developed from the statement of the problem and how hypotheses are developed from the research question, the statement of the problem, and the subproblems. Finally, the chapter will address assumptions and delimitations and how they are developed.

The Importance of Chapter One Core Sections

The core sections of Chapter One determine how the rest of the thesis will be written. They form the framework around which the rest of the paper will be developed. Chapter One can be likened to the frame of a building; it determines the size and the shape of each room. In a similar manner, the research question, the hypotheses, the objectives, and the subobjectives determine the size and shape of the thesis.

The Downward Importance Flow in Chapter One

The degree of importance of each of the key sections in Chapter One flows downward from the research question. The most important element in the research paper is the research question. It determines all major factors throughout the thesis. Next is the hypothesis (or hypotheses). The hypotheses help to determine the problem and subproblems. They in turn affect the research instrument questions, the areas to be analyzed in Chapter Four, and the data needed to determine thesis outcomes. The problems and subproblems identify the specific concerns addressed by the thesis. The definition of terms and abbreviations and the delimitations narrow the focus of the study, and the importance of the study examines why it is being undertaken in the first place.

The Final Research Question

The final research question is the most important part of the thesis. It is usually rewritten several times, and it is not unusual for a thesis writer to change research questions completely after undertaking a literature review. This may occur for several reasons. One is that you may find that there has been little written in the past on the subject and that obtaining data is extremely difficult. Although this alone should not discourage you, it may signify other problems.

A greater problem is that the thesis may be undoable; for one reason or another, completing the thesis may not be possible. One of the reasons for this is that identifying a population base from which it is practical to obtain data may be impossible. For example, the population may be too narrow or too broad, or it may be that the members in the population cannot be expected to respond to a questionnaire. Or the research question itself may be too nebulous. Questionnaire responses may be so broad and inconsistent that no meaningful results can be gained.

There are many possible problems. Narrow your research question, test it by asking it of sample groups, and explicitly define your key words, and your potential for developing a good thesis will increase.

The Statement of the Problem

The statement of the problem is essentially a rewording of the research question into a statement format. This allows you to see the research question from a different viewpoint. It also makes it easier to prepare subproblems, and it may help you identify key words and phrases to assist in your literature review.

Some research questions lend themselves to an easy conversion to problem statements; they are simply reworded. More often, however, it requires adding or taking away words, but you should try to work with essentially the same words and phrases that are in your research question. Look at the examples in Figure 4.1 and note in each case how the researcher changed the research question into a statement of the problem.

Draft a statement of the problem based on the research question and then review it several times, making any necessary changes. You may want to leave the original draft of the statement of the problem for several days, and then look at it from a fresh viewpoint. This approach may help you create a better statement of the problem.

RESEARCH QUESTION NUMBER ONE:
Has the installation of a window between the dining room and the kitchen increased sales in the 50-seat or less sit-down restaurants in the state of Florida that have installed such windows?

PROBLEM STATEMENT NUMBER ONE:
This study is designed to determine whether or not the installation of a window between the dining room and the kitchen of 50-seat or less sit-down restaurants located in the state of Florida has increased sales in those restaurants.

RESEARCH QUESTION NUMBER TWO:
Do the patrons of downtown all-suite hotels in Seattle prefer that hotel gift shops be located near the check-in desk or in some other location of the property?

PROBLEM STATEMENT NUMBER TWO:
This thesis will find out if the patrons of Seattle's all-suite hotels prefer for the gift shop to be located near the check-in desk, or if they prefer the gift shop to be located in some other location of the property.

RESEARCH QUESTION NUMBER THREE:
Are resort marketing directors in the state of West Virginia directing more of their marketing financial resources toward attracting guests originating from outside the United States today than they did in 1980?

Figure 4.1
Changes of research question to statement of the problem

PROBLEM STATEMENT NUMBER THREE:
Determining whether the marketing directors of West Virginia resorts are directing more of their marketing financial resources toward attracting guests originating from outside the United States today than they did in 1980 is the subject of this research.

The Subproblems

The subproblems are based directly on the problem and indirectly on the research question. In developing the subproblems, ask yourself: "What are the most important concerns or questions that make up this problem?"

Keep in mind that the subproblems form the nucleus of and the foundation for the research itself. The research instrument will elicit responses that are directly related to each of the subproblems.

By obtaining answers to the research instrument items that relate to each subproblem, answers to the subproblems themselves can be determined, usually through either inductive or deductive reasoning. Keep this in mind when developing the subproblems.

Look at Figure 4.2. Each researcher has developed subproblems that directly relate to the research question. Note that when the subproblems are resolved, an answer to the research question should clearly stand out.

One of the goals you should have when developing subproblems is the ability to clearly identify for the reader an answer to the subproblem based on the research instrument items. If the subproblem is stated in such a nebulous way that no concrete answer can be expected or research instrument items based on the subproblem cannot be devised, then the subproblem should be rewritten or at least reconsidered. Keep in mind

RESEARCH QUESTION NUMBER ONE:
Do the patrons of downtown all-suite hotels in Seattle prefer that hotel gift shops be located near the check-in desk or in some other location of the property?

SUBPROBLEM NUMBER ONE:
To what extent do downtown all-suite hotels in Seattle have hotel gift shops located near the check-in desk, and to what extent do they have them located in other locations of the property?

SUBPROBLEM NUMBER TWO:
What gift shop location preference data have been developed by downtown all-suite hotels in Seattle in either their preconstruction or their postconstruction research?

SUBPROBLEM NUMBER THREE:
Are there preference differences between customer types or categories regarding the location of gift shops in downtown all-suite hotels in Seattle?

SUBPROBLEM NUMBER FOUR:
Is it possible that the patrons of downtown all-suite hotels in Seattle do not care where the hotel gift shops are located?

RESEARCH QUESTION NUMBER TWO:
Are resort marketing directors in the state of West Virginia directing more of their marketing financial resources toward attracting guests originating from outside the United States today than they did in 1980?

SUBPROBLEM NUMBER ONE:
Do resort marketing directors in the state of West Virginia control the direction of their marketing financial resources?

Figure 4.2
Examples of subproblems developed from research questions

SUBPROBLEM NUMBER TWO:
Can West Virginia resort marketing directors obtain statistically comparable data on the direction of their marketing financial resources for the year 1980 and for the current year, and are they willing to provide these data accurately for the purpose of this study?

that research instrument items will need to be formulated for each subproblem. These research instrument items (normally questions) must be such that, when answered, one or more solutions to the subproblems result.

Hypotheses

A hypothesis is an educated guess regarding an outcome. When writing a thesis, you are expected to state one or more hypotheses in Chapter One. Through the research study (in Chapters Four and Five), you either prove the validity of the hypotheses or prove that the hypotheses are incorrect.

Review the examples of hypotheses presented in Figure 4.3. Notice how these hypotheses act as positive or negative projected answers to their corresponding research questions.

RESEARCH QUESTION NUMBER ONE:
Has the installation of a window between the dining room and the kitchen increased sales in the 50-seat or less sit-down restaurants in the state of Florida that have installed such windows?

HYPOTHESIS NUMBER ONE RELATING
TO RESEARCH QUESTION ONE:
It will be found that the installation of a window between the dining room and the kitchen has not increased sales in the 50-seat or less sit-down restaurants in the state of Florida that have installed such windows.

RESEARCH QUESTION NUMBER TWO:
Do the patrons of downtown all-suite hotels in Seattle prefer that hotel gift shops be located near the check-in desk or in some other location of the property?

HYPOTHESIS NUMBER ONE RELATING
TO RESEARCH QUESTION TWO:
It is hypothesized that patrons of downtown all-suite hotels in Seattle do not care where the hotel gift shop is located, as long as it is conveniently located on the property.

RESEARCH QUESTION NUMBER THREE:
Are resort marketing directors in the state of West Virginia directing more of their marketing financial resources toward attracting guests originating from outside the United States today than they did in 1980?

Figure 4.3
Examples of the relationship between hypotheses and research questions

HYPOTHESIS NUMBER ONE RELATING
TO RESEARCH QUESTION THREE:
Resort marketing directors in the state of West Virginia are directing more of their marketing financial resources toward attracting guests originating from outside the United States today than they did in 1980.

Many academicians feel that only a null hypothesis should be used in formal thesis writing. A null hypothesis predicts neither a positive nor a negative outcome; it states that the outcome will be one of the two or neither of the two. Few outcomes are right on the line between negative and positive, so many people reject the null hypothesis as being too hypothetical. Check with your professor to determine whether or not a null hypothesis will be expected.

Once one or more hypotheses have been postulated, explain them. This usually takes no more than one paragraph per hypothesis, but it can help clarify potential misunderstandings.

Organization of the Paper

In Chapter One, a one- or two-paragraph section tells the reader how the paper will be organized. It notes that the paper will be developed through five chapters, and it briefly discusses what the reader can expect to find in each chapter. Although the chapter contents are standard with all theses (with some leeway as it relates to optional material), the discussion of the chapter contents should be tailored to the individual thesis being prepared. For example, instead of just telling the reader that the thesis is based on the descriptive survey method (the method adopted by most who do research in the hospitality industry), give a brief explanation as to why this method has been adopted for your thesis and why it is more appropriate than other methods for your research question.

Keep in mind that this is just a first draft; you will probably make substantial changes as additional drafts are completed. However, even to do this first draft it would be wise to glance through the later chapters of this book to get a feel for how your paper will be organized. Read the summaries of each chapter, and whenever you are not sure you have a good feel for a particular section or part of the thesis, read that chapter in detail. This should help you write the first draft of the "Organization of the Paper."

Assumptions

Assumptions reduce potential criticism of the research and they help isolate the factors being tested or considered. Assumptions are a set of conditions that you presume apply, whether or not they really do. In stating assumptions, you are stating that these are factors that you presume are true and valid as they act on the condition or situation being studied. The study does not explore these assumptions. For example, it may be assumed that a significant number of respondents will be those to whom the research instrument and cover letter are addressed. It is usually also assumed, therefore, that the people responding are those who were addressed, and that they are providing accurate information as far as they are able to do so. These assumptions may or may not be valid. For example, when research instruments are sent to hotel general managers, many of the responses may actually be prepared by the general manager's secretary. Nevertheless, the thesis may include an assumption that states: "It is assumed that all or all but an insignificant number of the responses to the research instrument (questionnaire) on which this study is based will be prepared by the general managers to whom the research instrument cover letters are addressed."

There are, of course, many other assumptions that are made in studies. They too may or may not be valid. Study the assumption examples listed in Figure 4.4. They should give you a good idea how to formulate your assumptions.

Delimitations

Delimitations are acceptable limitations. Essentially, delimitations are restrictions placed on the study to make it doable.

One of the most common delimitations relates to the population surveyed. If cost, time, or other constraints prevent you from sampling the entire population, you can sample a portion of the population and state in the delimitations that only a portion of the population will be sampled. For example, if you want to find out staffing/turnover ratios at full-service restaurants, you might determine that a survey sent to full-service restaurant owners and managers (asking such questions as how many wait staff are employed, how many tables are in the establishment, and how many turnovers per breakfast, lunch, and dinner are averaged) would be a good way to approach the research. However, there are a large number of full-service restaurants in the world. At the very least, you would want to delimit the study to a survey of full-service restaurants in the United States, Canada, or some other country. Even with this delimitation, the population may still be so large that sampling it is prohibitive in terms of both cost and time. You could further delimit the population to a sampling of full-service restaurants in several states.

In addition to delimiting population, other appropriate delimitations should be considered. These should also be addressed in this section of Chapter One.

1. It is assumed that there are 50-seat or less sit-down restaurants in the state of Florida that have installed windows between the dining room and the kitchen.

2. It is assumed that the owners and managers who will be surveyed will have sales figures covering one or more years prior to and for all years after the installation of a window between the dining room and the kitchen.

3. It is assumed that the owners and managers who will be surveyed know how to calculate sales figures, will be willing to calculate sales figures, will be willing to release the calculated sales figures, and will calculate the sales figures in the same way for the years prior to the installation of a window between the dining room and the kitchen as for the years after the installation of the window.

4. It is assumed that resort marketing directors in the state of West Virginia direct their marketing financial resources.

5. It is assumed that resort marketing directors in the state of West Virginia can and do measure the amount of their financial resources in such a way that a calculation of the amount of financial resources directed toward attracting guests originating from ouside the United States and the amount of financial resources directed toward attracting guests originating from inside the United States can be measured and can accurately be compared.

Figure 4.4
Examples of
assumptions

6. It is assumed that records relating to the amount of financial resources directed to attracting guests originating from inside the United States and from outside the United States have been maintained by resort marketing directors in the state of West Virginia since 1979 and that the form of calculating and reporting these records has not changed since 1979.

Delimitations may relate to people and things. For example, a study of effective portion control might be delimited to servers only, excluding buyers, cooks, and other food handlers. It might also be limited to a consideration of serving containers, not including cooking utensils, serving utensils, and plates. Usually, the more specific you are when addressing delimitations, the better.

Look at the wide range of delimitations seen in the delimitation examples in Figure 4.5. They should give you some indication of the scope of thesis delimitations.

Summary

The core of Chapter One includes the research question, the statement of the problem, subproblems, hypotheses, a section on the organization of the paper, terms and abbreviations, assumptions, delimitations, and a section relating to the importance of the study. This chapter and the next one discuss these ingredients.

The research question is the most important element of Chapter One; all aspects of Chapter One relate to the research question. In fact, the entire thesis revolves around the research question.

Chapter One is sequenced to create a downward importance flow, from the research question down to the delimitations. Most theses include a section on the

1.   Fifty-seat or less sit-down restaurants in the state of Florida with windows between the dining room and the kitchen that were installed at the time the restaurant was built will not be considered in this study.

2.   Fifty-seat or less sit-down restaurants in the state of Florida that are not listed on the Florida Restaurant Association's list *State Sit-Down Restaurants* will not be considered in this study.

3.   The patrons of downtown all-suite hotels in Seattle will be limited to those persons who have rented rooms in these hotels and will not include those who may or may not be using one or more of the services of the hotels, but who have not checked into and/or are renting hotel rooms in one or more of the hotels.

4.   The downtown all-suite hotels in the city of Seattle will be limited to those listed as all-suite hotels in the listings of downtown hotels compiled and published by the Seattle Convention Bureau and the Downtown Seattle Chamber of Commerce.

Figure 4.5
Examples of delimitations

5.   The preferences of patrons of downtown all-suite hotels in Seattle that do not have hotel gift shops will not be considered in this study.

importance of the study after the delimitations, but a few academicians prefer that this section be placed right after the introduction to Chapter One and the paragraphs that discuss the research question.

Considerable thought must be given to the research question itself. Your research question must be doable, and you should be vitally interested in it. Your results must contribute to the industry.

The statement of the problem is similar to the research question. Subproblems grow out of the research question and the statement of the problem. There are usually at least three subproblems. Hypotheses are educated guesses stating outcome probabilities. These are either positive or negative statements, but a null hypothesis is preferred by some academicians.

One of the more difficult sections to write if you are new to researching and developing a thesis is the section on the organization of the paper. This is a vital part of Chapter One, but it is usually composed of no more than two or three paragraphs. The organization of the paper describes how the thesis will flow and gives an overview of the contents of each chapter. Avoid the temptation of making it purely mechanical, and make certain that the unique attributes of your thesis are brought out.

The "Assumptions" section identifies the major assumptions you have made. They are similar to delimitations, which identify those acceptable limitations of the study within which you plan to work (because of such constraints as cost, time, or accessibility).

The next chapter discusses the balance of the core ingredients for Chapter One, including a section on the organization of Chapter One and a section relating to the definition of terms and abbreviations. It also includes a section devoted to the "Importance of the Study" section of Chapter One.

Discussion Questions

These questions may be discussed by two or more students after class, or they may be discussed during class for a more wide-ranging discussion.

1. What can be likened to the frame of a building?

2. How are assumptions and delimitations similar?

3. In what order does the downward flow of importance in Chapter One occur (what comes first, second, and so on)?

4. In the "Organization of the Paper" section of Chapter One, what temptation should you avoid, and what kind of attributes should you make certain are brought out?

5. What is one of the reasons discussed in this chapter why it is not unusual for a thesis writer to change research questions completely after undertaking a literature review?

6. Based on having the research question to work with, how do you prepare the statement of the problem?

7. In what part of Chapter One do you usually find the "Importance of the Study" section? Where in Chapter One do some academicians prefer that the "Importance of the Study" section appear?

8. On what are the subproblems based directly, and on what are they based indirectly?

9. What do you reduce when you delimit the population that is worked with in the thesis?

10. What do assumptions reduce, and what do they help to isolate?

Role Play Exercises

Two students may participate in these role play exercises either outside of class or as in-class exercises. One plays the role of the first student and the other plays the role of the second student. Read the scripts and then pick up the conversations in your own words.

1. FIRST STUDENT: The instructor said that everything in Chapter One flows downward from the research question. What does this mean?

   SECOND STUDENT: The research question is the focus of the thesis. Everything else comes back to the research question and develops from it. Starting with the research question you can develop each of the other parts of Chapter One. As each additional component of Chapter One is completed it becomes a little easier to prepare the next ones. In other words, you start with the research question and then you...

   ### Continue on Your Own

2. FIRST STUDENT: I really don't understand this concept of "core sections." What are core sections? What are the other sections that are not core sections?

   SECOND STUDENT: Let's take one question at a time. The core sections are those around which...

   ### Continue on Your Own

3. FIRST STUDENT: There seems to be a strong tie between the statement of the problem, the subproblems, and the research question. How do these

interrelate and how are they mutually dependent upon one another, if in fact they are mutually dependent?

SECOND STUDENT: Your observation of the apparent interrelationship is an astute one. Yes, they are interrelated. Perhaps the closest interrelationship is between the...

Continue on Your Own

4.1. Research Question/Statement of the Problem/Subproblems

Type your name at the top of the next page. In the spaces provided, type (double-spaced) the information called for. This information consists of three components of Chapter One. They are: (1) your research question; (2) the statement of the problem for your thesis; and (3) three subproblems for your thesis. (Be sure to retain a copy of the completed exercise; you will need it to complete future exercises.)

Before handing in this assignment, review the information in this and previous chapters relating to these components of Chapter One, and study the examples provided. Remember that each word establishes or changes the meaning to some degree. Make sure you write what you mean and mean what you write.

To the completed assignment sheet, attach an Instructor Comment Sheet. Make sure the Instructor Comment Sheet has the Assignment section filled in and that it has your name on it. Place the assignment sheet and the Instructor Comment Sheet into an 8.5" × 11" manila envelope with a clasp flap with your name typed on the front of the envelope. If your instructor requests it, include a blank, top-quality audiotape (30 minutes long) with your name printed on it, so that your professor may give you feedback.

Research Question/Statement of the Problem/Three Subproblems

1. Research question: _____

   _____

2. Statement of the problem: _____

   _____

3. Three subproblems: _____

   A. Subproblem number one: _____

   _____

   _____

   B. Subproblem number two: _____

   _____

   _____

   C. Subproblem number three: _____

   _____

   _____

4.2. Three Hypotheses

Type your name at the top of the next page. In the spaces provided, type (double-spaced) the information called for: your research question and three hypotheses relating to projected outcomes of your research. (Be sure to retain a copy of the completed exercise; you will need it to complete future exercises.)

Before handing in this assignment, review the information in this chapter and your research relating to hypotheses. Study the examples provided. Remember that each word establishes or changes the meaning to some degree. Write what you mean and mean what you write.

To the completed listing of hypotheses, attach an Instructor Comment Sheet. Make sure the Instructor Comment Sheet has the Assignment section filled in and that it has your name on it. Place the assignment sheet and the Instructor Comment Sheet into an 8.5" × 11" manila envelope with a clasp flap with your name typed on the front of the envelope. If your instructor requests it, include a blank, top-quality audiotape (30 minutes long) with your name printed on it, so that your professor may give you feedback.

Three Hypotheses

Research question: _____

_____

1. Hypothesis number one: _____

_____

2. Hypothesis number two: _____

_____

3. Hypothesis number three: _____

_____

4.3. Four Assumptions and Four Delimitations

Type your name at the top of the next page. In the spaces provided, type (double-spaced) the information called for: your research question, four assumptions, and four delimitations.

Before handing in this assignment, review the information in this chapter and your research relating to assumptions and delimitations. Remember that each word establishes or changes the meaning to some degree.

Write an initial draft of the assumptions and delimitations, let it sit for a day or two, and then go back to it. Read your assumptions and delimitations, asking yourself if what you have written is really what you mean and ask yourself if these are the best assumptions and delimitations for your thesis. Then make any changes that you feel are needed before typing the assignment page. You may even want to review your work two or three times before handing it in.

To the completed listings of assumptions and delimitations, attach an Instructor Comment Sheet. Make sure the Instructor Comment Sheet has the Assignment section filled in and that it has your name on it. Place the assignment sheet and the Instructor Comment Sheet into an 8.5" × 11" manila envelope with a clasp flap with your name typed on the front of the envelope. If your instructor requests it, include a blank, top-quality audiotape (30 minutes long) with your name printed on it, so that your professor may give you feedback.

Four Assumptions and Four Delimitations

Research question: _____

1. Assumption number one: _____

_____

2. Assumption number two: _____

_____

3. Assumption number three: _____

_____

4. Assumption number four: _____

_____

5. Delimitation number one: _____

_____

6. Delimitation number two: _____

_____

7. Delimitation number three: _____

_____

8. Delimitation number four: _____

CHAPTER FIVE

_____

Completing Chapter One

*U*pon *completion of this chapter, you will be able to:*

1. List the flow of sections for Chapter One.

2. Write an initial draft of the "Terms and Abbreviations" section of Chapter One.

3. Prepare a paragraph on the "Organization of the Paper" section of Chapter One.

4. Discuss at least three approaches that can be used in establishing the importance of the study.

Introduction

In completing Chapter One, you start by reviewing the organizational structure. Review each section of Chapter One and be aware of how they fit together. After the structure is exactly as you want it, draft out the "Structure" section of Chapter One, and insert it after the introduction and before the section titled "The Research Question."

Next, go back to the note cards that you prepared earlier. Pull out the cards titled "Terms" and "Abbreviations." Organize them alphabetically and draft a "Terms and Abbreviations" section.

The writing of the "Importance of the Study" section comes next. This is usually done after you develop a list of points you consider important. Based on this list, prepare an outline, and write the section from the outline.

The final section of Chapter One to be written is the summary. This is drafted after reviewing all of the previously written sections of Chapter One. It will be revised after the final draft has been completed. After rereading Chapters One and Two, revise the summary to tie the chapters together.

The Final Organizational Structure of Chapter One

The flow of Chapter One has been dictated by tradition. The titles of each section, in order, are as follows: (1) Chapter One Title Page, (2) Introduction, (3) Structure,

(4) The Research Question, (5) Statement of the Problem, (6) Subproblems, (7) Hypotheses, (8) Organization, (9) Definitions of Terms and Abbreviations, (10) Assumptions, (11) Delimitations, (12) Importance of the Study, (13) Summary, (14) Footnotes, and (15) Bibliography. It is necessary to have a smooth transition from one section to the next. Although this is not easy (sometimes it is impossible) to accomplish, the use of transition sentences will help the reader make an easy transition. Many of these can be written as the drafts are prepared, but it is usually necessary to set the manuscript aside for two or three days and then reread it, inserting more or different transition sentences.

Defining Terms and Abbreviations

The terms and abbreviations used throughout the thesis should be defined in this section. It is especially important to define all key words and phrases found in the research question. In addition, there will be words, phrases, or acronyms used throughout the paper that may be unfamiliar or may be interpreted in more than one way. Each of these should be included in the definitions of terms and abbreviations.

Most of the terms, abbreviations, acronyms, and phrases that will need to be defined will appear in Chapter Two. Keep note cards of these; list them as you come across them or develop them. An easy way to do this is to put them on note cards that are a different color than the note cards used for the other references. As you find definitions, abbreviations, terms, acronyms, and phrases defined in the literature during the review of literature conducted for Chapter Two, write the definitions on the appropriate note cards, and reference the sources. In other cases, a dictionary definition will be appropriate. Some terms you may define yourself; give considerable thought to the parameters of these self-defined terms.

Review the definitions of terms and abbreviations provided in Figure 5.1 and note how the author weaves together dictionary definitions, "expert" definitions, and "self-defined" definitions. Acronyms and phrases are mixed in with single-word definitions. Note that the author provides a list of abbreviations after the definitions. Separating the abbreviations from the definitions is usually not required, and some academicians mandate that it *not* be done. However, when abbreviations are listed separately, the reader is often able to locate them more easily.

Keep in mind that new terms, acronyms, and phrases will be encountered in the writing of Chapters Three, Four, Five, and the appendixes. These should be added to the "Terms and Abbreviations" section of Chapter One, and the section should be brought up to date before the final bound copies of the thesis are turned in for a grade. If you do this, the reader who encounters a new term, acronym, or phrase at the end of the thesis will be able to refer back to the "Terms and Abbreviations" section of Chapter One.

Writing the "Importance of the Study" Section

Many students encounter problems when writing the "Importance of the Study" section. There tends to be a belief on the part of some students that because the student feels that the subject is important, it is important, and therefore the reader should "automatically" recognize that importance. Unfortunately, some topics simply are not important. In a typical class, a large percentage of the students will select topics that are not considered important by the professor. Some students go as far as to undertake research into Chapter Two to find justification for their belief that their research question is important. This can be a good approach. It is the responsibility of the student to convince the professor that the topic is important. Make it a point to do some "impor-

DEFINITIONS OF TERMS

Wines by-the-glass: Those wines offered by the bottle, jug, or box that may be sold as a single glass.

Half-bottles: Half as much as the standard 750 ml bottle, these smaller wine bottles contain 375 ml of wine, or just over two glasses.

Wine list: A grouping of wines by color, region, or style; offered by the restaurant for sale.

Varietals: A specific grape variety used to make the wine listed on the label. Cabernet or Chardonnay rather than red or white. (A definition provided by Professor Ray Langbeuh, Chair, HMTA Department, Metropolitan State College, Denver, Colorado.)

Sommelier: A waiter in a restaurant who has charge of wines and their service; a wine steward. (*Webster's New Collegiate Dictionary*, G. & C. Merriam Co., Springfield, Mass., 1975, p. 1108.)

ABBREVIATIONS AND ACRONYMS

W.C.I.: The Western Culinary Institute.

C.I.A.: The Culinary Institute of America.

Figure 5.1 Examples of definitions of terms. *Modified MSCD HMTA Thesis Component. Reproduced with permission.*

tance" checks with your professor early on in your research, and continue to get feedback as you refine your research question.

One of the best ways of approaching the "Importance of the Study" section is to prepare a list of reasons why you believe the topic is important to those working in the industry. If these reasons can be backed up by literature references, your case will be considerably stronger.

An excellent approach is to view the concept of research (that is, the thesis) as "problem solving." If the thesis is centered around finding a solution to an industry problem and that problem is well documented, the "Importance of the Study" section will be easy to write and to justify.

Doctoral dissertations usually conclude with recommendations for further research. You may find quotes emphasizing the need to do further research in published dissertations that are related to your subject. These should be sought while preparing Chapter Two. Start with *Dissertation Abstracts* and then review the entire dissertation (especially the concluding recommendations) when you find promising references.

Interviews in trade publications and industry studies sometimes identify problems. Industry experts being interviewed will sometimes state that additional research is needed in a particular area. This type of reference should be sought out during the research undertaken to write Chapter Two. It should be quoted in the "Importance of the Study" section.

You can back up your belief in the importance of your research question by conducting sample surveys of a small target group of industry experts. These surveys ask whether or not the experts consider the topic to be important and, if so, why. If this type of survey is done well, it can lend considerable credibility to your claim that the topic is important.

Study Figure 5.2. Note the directness of the writing. There is no beating around the bush and there is little editorialism. The author simply, clearly, and precisely states his case and backs it up with hard evidence.

According to this year's *Las Vegas Prospective Market Survey*, approximately 20% of sales for Las Vegas hotels comes from the Japanese. This is a substantial amount. However, research indicates that no comprehensive study has been conducted in Japanese of Japanese asking why they choose to visit Las Vegas. Twenty-five Las Vegas hotel marketing executives spoken with in a preliminary telephone survey indicated their marketing to the Japanese market was: (1) directed to inbound tour operators only; (2) based on general, rather than Japanese-targeted studies; or (3) based on public relations company projections. None had ever seen a survey of Las Vegas-bound Japanese tourists. More importantly, all but two of the 25 hotel marketing executives indicated that the results of such a study would be considered very useful. It would, they indicated, help them to more directly tailor their marketing and it should help them to obtain: (1) a better return-on-investment for their marketing expenses spent on attracting Japanese tourists; (2) more Japanese tourists; (3) more effective marketing programs targeted to Japanese tourists; (4) a better repeat factor with more Japanese returning to Las Vegas; and (5) a longer average Japanese tourist stay and a larger per Japanese stay-in-hotel expenditure.

Figure 5.2
Importance of the study example. *Modified MSCD HMTA Thesis component. Reproduced with permission.*

In whatever way you prepare this section, you should be aware that it is a critical section. The acceptance of the study as a whole depends on your ability to make a case for the importance of your topic.

Writing the Chapter One Summary

In writing the summary of Chapter One, two things are important. The first is to give a brief synopsis of the major points in each section of Chapter One. The second is to provide an introduction or transition to Chapter Two.

One of the easiest ways to accomplish the first objective is to reread each section in Chapter One and summarize what that section has to say in one or two sentences. After the sentences have been written, write them in paragraph form in the same order in which they were prepared (that is, from the sentence relating to the first section to the sentence relating to the last section).

The resulting paragraph may be stilted and read rather strangely. Smooth out the rough points, adding or taking away words, phrases, and perhaps even sentences until you have a smooth flow from one concept to the next. It may be necessary to divide this paragraph into two paragraphs, but your goal should be one short, concise paragraph.

The job is not over, however, when this summary paragraph is written. Next, you have to write a transition paragraph to introduce Chapter Two.

Tying in Chapters One and Two

The final paragraph in Chapter One—the end of the "Summary" section—is a transition paragraph that ties together Chapters One and Two. It is used to show the relationship between the two chapters, to conclude Chapter One, and to introduce Chapter Two. This paragraph is the most formal structure that ties together the two chapters, but it is not the only section that ties them together. It should concentrate on the relationships between Chapters One and Two and should introduce the reader to the fact that Chapter One is complete and that Chapter Two, the literature review, is next. It should be clearly pointed out that Chapter Two is designed to reinforce Chapter One and to tell the reader about research relating to the subject area and what the outcomes of this research are.

Throughout both Chapters One and Two, however, there need to be cross-references. This is especially true as it relates to specific sections of Chapter One, which tie in closely to Chapter Two. As the sections in Chapter One are written, appropriate references to Chapter Two should be made. As sections of Chapter Two are written that have a direct bearing on Chapter One, appropriate references to Chapter One should be made. This cross-referencing can apply to almost all sections of Chapter One, but it usually applies most clearly with the following sections: (1) "Definitions of Terms and Abbreviations," (2) "The Research Question," (3) "Importance of the Study," (4) "Assumptions," and (5) "Delimitations."

Summary

The organizational structure of Chapter One is considered in this chapter. The structure is dictated by tradition, although there are some possible variations. The essential structure is as follows: (1) the Chapter One title page, (2) the introduction, (3) the structure, (4) the research question, (5) the statement of the problem, (6) the subproblems, (7) the hypotheses, (8) the organization, (9) the definitions of terms and abbreviations, (10) the assumptions, (11) the delimitations, (12) the importance of the study, (13) the summary of the chapter, (14) chapter footnotes, and (15) the chapter bibliography. It is important to have a smooth transition from one section to another.

This chapter also discussed the writing of the "Terms and Abbreviations" section of Chapter One. This is done directly from the note cards you made during the researching of Chapter Two and the preparation of Chapter One. Keep in mind that new terms and abbreviations will be encountered in the writing of each chapter, and therefore this section of Chapter One should be continuously updated.

The "Importance of the Study" section is perhaps the most important section in Chapter One; if you are unable to establish the importance of the study, your research question will need to be changed. Prepare a list of reasons why the study is important. Documentation from the literature can be helpful; this could come from dissertation references, quotes in interviews that appear in trade publications, or sample surveys.

The last part of this chapter discusses the Chapter One summary. The summary is a brief synopsis of the major points in each section of Chapter One; it should be no longer than one or two paragraphs. It should conclude with a short paragraph that introduces Chapter Two.

The relationship between Chapter One and Chapter Two should always be kept in mind. Cross-referencing between the chapters will allow the reader to see how individual subject areas within the chapters are treated and will provide a fuller understanding of each subject area. This especially applies to the following Chapter One sections: the definitions of terms and abbreviations, the research question, the importance of the study, the assumptions, and the delimitations.

Discussion Questions

These questions may be discussed by two or more students outside of class, or they may be discussed during class for a more wide-ranging discussion.

1. How do you start in preparing the completion of Chapter One?

2. To what five sections of Chapter One does cross-referencing between Chapter One and Chapter Two apply most clearly?

3. What is the order of sections in Chapter One?

4. What is the final paragraph in Chapter One, and what does it tie together?

5. What section of Chapter One contains definitions of terms, abbreviations, acronyms, and phrases that may be new to the reader?

6. In writing the summary of Chapter One, what two things are important?

7. How might the note cards used for defining terms, abbreviations, acronyms, and phrases differ from the note cards used for other references?

8. The acceptance of the study as a whole depends on your ability to make a case for what?

9. Why should the "Terms and Abbreviations" section of Chapter One be brought up to date before the thesis is turned in for a grade?

10. Who has the responsibility of convincing whom that the topic selected for the thesis is important?

Role Play Exercises

Two students may participate in these role play exercises either outside of class or as in-class exercises. One plays the role of the first student and the other plays the role of the second student. Read the scripts and then pick up the conversations in your own words.

1. **FIRST STUDENT:** I think my research question and my study are important. At least they are important to me.

   SECOND STUDENT: I am sure they are. But the real question is whether or not they are important to the hospitality industry, other researchers, or the public as a whole. If you can show the importance to one or more of these three, the chances are our professor will agree.

   FIRST STUDENT: It may or may not be important to those people. I just don't understand why it should be.

   SECOND STUDENT: Let me explain why thesis subjects need to be considered important by people other than the student who undertakes the thesis research. Then I'll tell you about some research you can do to back up your claim that your thesis question is important. Let me start by . . .

   ### Continue on Your Own

2. **FIRST STUDENT:** From a reading of this chapter it appears that work on the definitions of terms and abbreviations is never finished.

   SECOND STUDENT: It does seem so.

   FIRST STUDENT: It seems like a lot of effort to have to continue to work on this section even after Chapter One is finished. I really don't know why I should have to go to so much trouble.

   SECOND STUDENT: It does take more effort than it would if you just completed Chapter One, set it aside, and considered the whole chapter to be totally finished. However, continuing work on the terms and abbreviations section is needed. In fact it is essential because . . .

   ### Continue on Your Own

3. **FIRST STUDENT:** The Chapter One summary seems like a big waste of time. Why have a summary at all and why should I even consider Chapter Two when I'm working on Chapter One?

SECOND STUDENT: The summary is a logical conclusion to the chapter. There is a strong relationship between the first and second chapter. Let me give you some easy hints on how to prepare the summary and then I'll explain what the interrelationships are between the two chapters and why it is necessary to constantly identify these relationships. Let's start with...

Continue on Your Own

5.1. Organization of the Paper

Review the section on the organization of the paper in Chapter 5 of this book and prepare a draft of the "Organization of the Paper" section of Chapter One of your thesis. You may wish to review the chapters about the writing of Chapter Three of the thesis (Chapters 8 through 10 of this book) first. Be sure to type your name at the top of each page of your "Organization of the Paper" draft.

To your completed draft of the organization of your paper, attach an Instructor Comment Sheet. Make sure the Instructor Comment Sheet has the Assignment section filled in and that it has your name on it. Place the organization of the paper draft and the Instructor Comment Sheet into an 8.5" × 11" manila envelope with a clasp flap with your name typed on the envelope. If your instructor requests it, include a blank, top-quality audiotape (30 minutes long) with your name printed on it, so that your professor may give you feedback.

5.2. Terms and Abbreviations

Review all that you have written so far. Wherever you encounter a term, acronym, abbreviation, phrase, or other expression that might not be fully understood, prepare a note card providing a definition or explanation. Review the section on terms and abbreviations in this chapter. Prepare an initial draft of the "Terms and Abbreviations" section of Chapter One of your thesis.

To your completed draft of the terms and abbreviations section of your paper, attach an Instructor Comment Sheet. Make sure the Instructor Comment Sheet has the Assignment section filled in and that it has your name on it. Place the terms and abbreviations draft and the Instructor Comment Sheet into an 8.5" × 11" manila envelope with a clasp flap with your name typed on the envelope. If your instructor requests it, include a blank, top-quality audiotape (30 minutes long) with your name printed on it, so that your professor may give you feedback.

5.3. Importance of the Study

Review the section on the importance of the study in this chapter. Also review all material relating to the importance of your research question that you found in the literature review. Review the "Schematic of the Development Process in Writing the Importance of the Study." Based on these reviews, prepare an initial draft of the "Importance of the Study" section of Chapter One of your thesis.

To your completed draft of the "Importance of the Study" section of your paper, attach an Instructor Comment Sheet. Make sure the Instructor Comment Sheet has the Assignment section filled in and that it has your name on it. Place the "Importance of the Study" draft and the Instructor Comment Sheet into an 8.5" × 11" manila envelope with a clasp flap with your name typed on the envelope. If your instructor requests it, include a blank, top-quality audiotape (30 minutes long) with your name printed on it, so that your professor may give you feedback.

Schematic of the Development Process in Writing the Importance of the Study

Move from one step to the next by first identifying all benefiters (those individuals, groups, and organizations that would benefit from the completed study). For each benefiter or benefiter group identify reasons why your proposed study is or might be important. The next step is to identify how the benefits or potential benefits of your study will be communicated to each benefiter or benefiter group. Conclude this section of the chapter with a summary or a conclusion.

Step one	Step two	Step three	Step four
Identify benefiters or benefiter groups	Identify reason(s) why each benefiter or benefiter group will benefit from your study	Identify how the benefits or potential benefits will be communicated to each benefiter or benefiter group	Summarize or prepare some other type of conclusion
B-1	R-1, R-2, etc.	C-1, C-2, etc.	Summary
B-2	R-1, R-2, etc.	C-1, C-2, etc.	Summary
B-3	R-1, R-2, etc.	C-1, C-2, etc.	Summary
B-4	R-1, R-2, etc.	C-1, C-2, etc.	Summary
Etc.	Etc.	Etc.	Etc.

Note: The information in step three—the communicating benefits to each benefiter or benefiter group—will be used in writing a part of Chapter Five of your thesis. Save this data and refer to it when you start the preparation of Chapter Five.

5.4. First Draft of Chapter One

Review Chapters 3 through 5 of this book. Based on the information in these chapters and your own research, prepare an initial draft of Chapter One of your thesis. (Be sure to retain a copy of the completed exercise; you will need it to complete future exercises.)

Your draft should include at least the following: (1) the Chapter One title page, (2) an introduction to the chapter, (3) a section titled "Structure," (4) a section titled "The Research Question," (5) a section titled "The Statement of the Problem," (6) a section titled "Subproblems," (7) a section titled "Hypotheses," (8) a section titled "Organization," (9) a section titled "Definitions of Terms and Abbreviations," (10) a section titled "Assumptions," (11) a section titled "Delimitations," (12) a section titled "The Importance of the Study," (13) the summary of the chapter, (14) chapter footnotes, and (15) the chapter bibliography. Make certain that there are smooth transitions between sections. Be sure to type your name at the top of each page.

To your completed initial draft of Chapter One, attach an Instructor Comment Sheet. Make sure the Instructor Comment Sheet has the Assignment section filled in and that it has your name on it. Place the initial draft of Chapter One and the Instructor Comment Sheet into an 8.5" × 11" manila envelope with a clasp flap with your name typed on the envelope. If your instructor requests it, include a blank, top-quality audio-tape (30 minutes long) with your name printed on it, so that your professor may give you feedback.

Chapter Two Revisited

U*pon completion of this chapter, you will be able to:*

1. Prepare a title page for Chapter Two of your thesis.

2. Compile a bibliography for Chapter Two of your thesis.

3. Explain why the preparation of the literature review is an ongoing effort.

4. Write a final paragraph or two for Chapter Two of your thesis that ties together Chapters One and Two and introduces Chapter Three.

Introduction

After Chapter One has been completed, it is time to go back to Chapter Two and complete it. As you have already discovered, there is a strong interrelationship between Chapters One and Two; they are written almost simultaneously and depend on one another to a considerable degree. Starting with Chapter Two, moving to Chapter One, and then moving back to Chapter Two tends to work well for most people new to thesis writing.

When Chapter Two was started, you did most of the developmental work, research work, and writing of drafts. At this time the final touches are added so that Chapter Two can be completed and set aside, at least temporarily, while Chapters Three through Five are developed.

You need to prepare front pages for Chapter Two, write an introduction, prepare footnotes, and develop a bibliography. The three main parts of Chapter Two—the introduction, body, and conclusion—should be reviewed and revised. Note that the introduction to the chapter may be different than the introductory portion of the main body of Chapter Two. The introductory section, which is titled "Introduction," usually introduces the concepts and the approaches that will be used in the chapter. When this is the case, the introduction to the main section of the paper (not titled "Introduction") tells the reader briefly that which will be discussed in detail in the body of the chapter.

The final part of Chapter Two will be a paragraph or two that ties together Chapters One and Two and introduces Chapter Three.

The Ongoing Literature Review Draft

Many educators who oversee thesis writing require that research for Chapter Two be ongoing; the search of the literature can take a considerable amount of time. In many cases, identifying a potentially good article, synopsis, or book in a resource publication is only the first step. It may take several weeks or months to obtain the material. Most complete literature reviews depend on obtaining material that is not available in your library, but must be borrowed from one or usually several libraries around the country. In some cases, materials must be purchased from research sources. This can be expensive and can take a long time. In addition, new articles or books relating to the thesis subject can be published during the time your work is being completed.

You should be able to expand your list of bibliographic references by searching for appropriate material in the bibliographies of the books and articles that you initially discover. Frequently, a single article's bibliography will give you four or five new publications of direct benefit to you. Some of these, in turn, will have bibliographies of their own that will lead you to still more pertinent data sources. Bibliographies can have a snowball effect.

All of this research takes time, however. It can seldom be accomplished in a few days or even in a few weeks. Many professors expect you to continue your research while you are writing Chapters Three, Four, and Five. Prior to completing the thesis, they expect you to go back to Chapter Two and update it.

Writing the Front Pages for Chapter Two

The front page for Chapter Two is usually only the title page. Some researchers, especially those who are working with very technical matters, will have listings of charts, graphs, and tables for Chapter Two in addition to an overall listing at the beginning of the thesis. This is rare, and is needed only when there are a substantial number of charts, graphs, and tables.

The title page for Chapter Two is similar to the one that was developed for Chapter One. Use the title "The Literature Review" or "The Review of Related Literature." (Check with your professor to determine whether or not your institution has a preference.) The title appears about a third of the way down the page, centered. (See Figure 6.1.)

Writing the Introduction to Chapter Two

The introductory section of Chapter Two identifies what a literature review is and how it will be developed for the thesis at hand. Although the process is similar for all theses, you should expect that some readers may have little knowledge of what a literature review is and how it is prepared. You should identify both the print and nonprint sources searched. Provide overall evaluations regarding sources that would be expected to provide good references as well as those that may provide material, but might not readily come to mind. You should strive to convey the idea that a comprehensive search has been conducted.

In the introduction to Chapter Two you discuss what choices you made when writing the thesis and why. For example, identify which style manual you used, and explain the reasons why you used it.

If you use a unique or unusual data-gathering or data-processing approach, explain the approach, and explain why it was adopted. For example, suppose you find articles

REVIEW OF

RELATED LITERATURE

Figure 6.1
*Modified MSCD
HMTA Thesis
Component. Re-
produced with
permission.*

152

with data that you suspect may not be valid or may be strongly skewed. It is appropriate in the introduction to briefly point out that based on a suspicion, you feel that independent verification is needed. Provide the reasons for your suspicion. Then explain how the independent verification was obtained and why this particular approach was taken.

Here's an example. A study of compensation trends in the resort industry identified a fairly obscure title, and the literature review identified two salary surveys for those in the industry holding this title. The results of the two surveys were substantially different. This led the researcher to believe that there might be problems with one or both of the surveys. The researcher obtained as much data as possible about the surveys, but was unable to discover the problem because of a lack of information regarding how the surveys were conducted. The researcher decided to verify the results by sending out a questionnaire to those working in the industry. Her results were similar to one of the two studies. She concluded that her study and the study that reached similar results were probably more accurate, but without being able to obtain greater information there would be no way to determine what the problem was with the survey that found such substantially different results. She noted all this in Chapter Two of her thesis.

In another instance a researcher found that some of the primary data needed simply did not exist. The choice was between changing to a different study or gathering the data needed to complete the research. She decided to conduct primary research to obtain the information needed. In the end she developed the equivalent of two theses to accomplish the goals of one.

Revising Chapter Two to the Three Standard Sections

Start the initial draft of the main body of Chapter Two by sorting your note cards into the order designated by your outline. Write the body of the chapter from the notecards, in accordance with the outline.

Concepts are grouped and summarized. Always reference each concept or viewpoint discussed. If you do not, the reader can assume that it is *your* concept or viewpoint, and, as noted, editorialism is not supposed to be included in Chapter Two. In summarizing viewpoints and concepts, try to determine current thought and synthesize it. Avoid writing a series of statements such as "Smith said this," "Jones said that," and so on. Some of this is acceptable, but it should be kept to a minimum.

This process will provide a rough draft of Chapter Two. This needs to be polished. Reread the paragraphs you have written, making any appropriate changes. Organize the paragraphs into logical sections and divide them with subheadings that relate to the material covered in the paragraphs. The end result will be a somewhat polished body of Chapter Two, but it will still need to be surrounded by an introduction and a conclusion.

The introduction is a summary of what will follow and the conclusion is a summary of what came before. After reviewing the body of the material, the two summaries should be prepared, one with the purpose of introducing the material, the other with the purpose of reviewing it.

The Footnotes for Chapter Two

The footnotes for Chapter Two should be prepared in accordance with the guidelines specified in your style manual. Some style manuals call for the use of endnotes. Endnotes are references placed at the end of a chapter or book. They indicate the source of the quote or the information in the statement. If footnotes are used, they are placed at the bottom of the page on which they are cited. Endnotes are cited numerically throughout the text and are listed at the end of the chapter, after the summary and before the bibliography. When this is the case, it is helpful to write each note on a card the way it will appear in the endnote section. These cards can be prepared as the chapter is written, numbered sequentially in the order in which the footnotes appear. The advantage to having them on cards is that when you write the endnote section, you can type it directly from the information on the cards. In addition, if paragraphs of the chapter are switched from one place to another, the order of the endnotes will change. By having them on cards, you simply change the card number and the corresponding endnote number.

The Bibliography for Chapter Two

The bibliography for Chapter Two is prepared in much the same way as the footnotes. Slightly different information is included in the citation, however, and the bibliography is organized alphabetically by author. Most thesis researchers will find that by keeping $3" \times 5"$ bibliography cards (of a different color or kept in a separate file), it will be much easier to prepare the bibliography.

After Chapter Two has been completed, go back and identify each footnote and each section that has drawn on information for which a bibliography citation would be appropriate. The indexed bibliography cards can then be pulled and stacked. Place the cards in alphabetical order by the author's last name. The bibliography can be typed directly from the cards.

In preparing the bibliography, follow the examples and instructions provided in the style manual you have adopted. Some who are new to undertaking research find a bibliography model that they like in a different style manual and use it instead, but it is considered inappropriate in formal writing to use more than one style manual. Most professors feel strongly about not allowing the use of any source other than a single style manual.

Summary

In developing the first two chapters, it is beneficial to start with Chapter Two, move to Chapter One, and then go back to Chapter Two. The completion process for Chapter Two is discussed in this chapter.

At this stage you must go back and review the rough draft of Chapter Two, and you must write some additional sections: the Chapter Two title page, an introduction, footnotes, and a bibliography. One or two paragraphs need to be added to the conclusion to round out the chapter. These paragraphs tie together Chapters One and Two and introduce Chapter Three.

Chapter Two is still not finished. The literature review is an ongoing effort that will continue throughout the writing of the thesis. Because of time delays in getting information, Chapter Two may not be completed until right before the entire thesis is finished.

The front page of Chapter Two consists of the title page, and it is only one line long. That line reads either "The Literature Review" or "The Review of Related Literature."

The introductory section of Chapter Two explains what a literature review is and details how it will be developed. Print and nonprint sources that have been searched are identified, and choices you have made are noted and justified.

Polish the body of Chapter Two by a continuous process of rereading it, making changes, and setting it aside for future review. As it is polished, it is surrounded by the introductory and concluding sections.

The footnotes and bibliography are prepared by working from note cards. Use the guidelines found in your style manual in preparing the footnotes and the bibliography.

Be careful not to copy bibliographical references from a book; follow the style detailed in your style manual.

Discussion Questions

These questions may be discussed by two or more students outside of class, or they may be discussed during class for a more wide-ranging discussion.

1. In what way is the introduction to the chapter different than the introductory portion of the main body of Chapter Two?

2. Why should you not follow a bibliography model in a reference book when preparing the bibliography?

3. The final part of Chapter Two is one or two paragraphs. What do they do?

4. By what part of the bibliographical citation are bibliographical references alphabetically listed?

5. Why should research for Chapter Two be an ongoing effort?

6. What are two advantages of having footnote reference information on individual cards?

7. What are the two possible titles of Chapter Two?

8. In accordance with what guidelines should the footnotes for Chapter Two be prepared?

9. In addition to identifying the choices you have made in the introductory section to Chapter Two, what else should you point out?

10. Within the body of the chapter, where are footnote references placed, and what do they indicate?

Role Play Exercises

Two students may participate in these role play exercises either outside of class or as in-class exercises. One plays the role of the first student and the other plays the role of the second student. Read the scripts and then pick up the conversations in your own words.

1. **FIRST STUDENT:** I really don't see what the fuss is all about. Why can't I just throw together the beginning and ending parts of Chapter Two with the draft body that I completed earlier and hand this in?

   SECOND STUDENT: That *is* the first step in preparing a more polished draft of Chapter Two, but much more work is needed.

   FIRST STUDENT: What do you mean that much more work is needed? What else do I have to do?

   SECOND STUDENT: If you are going to come up with a top-quality second chapter, a process will need to be followed. This process is somewhat involved. It starts with . . .

   Continue on Your Own

2. **FIRST STUDENT:** It looks like there are several options open to me in preparing the footnotes.

    SECOND STUDENT: There are several options, but these are severely limited by the style manual you select. Each style manual limits you to only one type or process of footnoting.

    FIRST STUDENT: Well, what are my options and which option is best?

    SECOND STUDENT: The options are...

    ### Continue on Your Own

3. **FIRST STUDENT:** This chapter talks about two kinds of introductions and I guess I might need both. What is the difference and why might I need two of them?

    SECOND STUDENT: Both introductions are important, but they are different. One introduction...

    ### Continue on Your Own

6.1. Chapter Two Bibliography

Review the information in this chapter concerning the development of a bibliography for Chapter Two. Also review your style manual, your bibliography note cards, and your research relating to the writing of thesis bibliographies. Based on this information, prepare a Chapter Two bibliography. Type your name at the top of each page of the bibliography and follow the guidelines set out in your style manual.

To your completed bibliography, attach an Instructor Comment Sheet. Make sure the Instructor Comment Sheet has the Assignment section filled in and that it has your name on it. Place the bibliography and the Instructor Comment Sheet into an 8.5" × 11" manila envelope with a clasp flap with your name typed on the envelope. If your instructor requests it, include a blank, top-quality audiotape (30 minutes long) with your name printed on it, so that your professor may give you feedback.

6.2. Second Draft of Chapter Two

Review the following: (1) information in this chapter regarding the writing of Chapter Two; (2) information in Chapters 1 through 5 of this book regarding Chapter Two; (3) your first draft of Chapter Two; and (4) your instructor's comments regarding your first draft of Chapter Two. Based on these, prepare a second draft of Chapter Two. Be sure that it includes all required components and any optional components you wish to include. Type your name at the top of each page of this second draft.

To your completed second draft of Chapter Two, attach an Instructor Comment Sheet. Make sure the Instructor Comment Sheet has the Assignment section filled in and that it has your name on it. Place the second draft of Chapter Two and the Instructor Comment Sheet into an 8.5" × 11" manila envelope with a clasp flap with your name typed on the envelope. If your instructor requests it, include a blank, top-quality audiotape (30 minutes long) with your name printed on it, so that your professor may give you feedback.

CHAPTER SEVEN

The Cover Letter and the Research Instrument

U*pon completion of this chapter, you will be able to:*

1. Draft a research instrument cover letter appropriate for the thesis being developed.

2. Refine the first draft of Chapter One and prepare an updated second draft.

3. Complete at least 10 research instrument note cards.

4. Detail the process of responding to instructor critiques of thesis chapters and preparing for follow-up meetings with the instructor, at which revisions of critiqued material will be reviewed.

Introduction

There are some types of research for which questionnaires are inappropriate (legitimate data sources include experimentation, content analysis, observation, archival sources, and secondary data), but discussions with educators suggest that most of the theses written at the bachelor's degree level relating to the hospitality industry are founded on questionnaires (often called *research instruments*). Even when a questionnaire is not developed and mailed to a large number of potential respondents, a research instrument of some type is often used to gather and categorize data. For example, when a study is based on the Delphi technique (in which focus groups consider specific problems and the findings are compared), the results are usually summarized in a one- or two-page document that frequently is compared to a summary compiled from the use of a questionnaire.

This chapter will focus on the questionnaire and the cover letter that accompanies it. It will start by identifying the importance of the questionnaire and its role as a foundation for research. Next, the importance of joining the population and the research question to the research instrument will be discussed.

The bulk of this chapter will relate to the mechanics of developing the research instrument. This section will start with an analysis of research instrument development techniques. It will consider how note cards can be used to catalog questions, how interview sampling can be undertaken, and how focus group approaches can be used in developing research instrument questions.

The final part of the research instrument section of this chapter will be devoted to the process of writing the first draft of the research instrument. In this section, you will learn how to undertake similar question blocking and how to handle reworded question distribution. Note card question refining and the simplifying of wording will be addressed next. You will learn to: (1) relate instrument items to their research question; (2) relate instrument items to statistical treatments; and (3) relate instrument item outcomes to visual data displays.

The final section of the chapter will discuss the writing of the research instrument cover letter. Each section of the cover letter will be discussed, and an example will be provided.

The Questionnaire as a Foundation for Original Research

A thesis is intended to be original research; it is based on data that are original to the author and not secondary (that is, based solely or primarily on data found in the literature). Because the questionnaire is intended to be completed by a large number of experts in the field being studied, it is often a reaction survey. Statistics drawn from the survey form the foundation for conclusions. Since the questionnaire is developed by the thesis writer and is, therefore, "original" with the writer, the thesis itself (which is based on the results calculated from questionnaire responses) is considered original.

The Importance of Tieing the Population and the Thesis Research Question to the Research Instrument

It would appear obvious that the thesis research question should tie in directly with the questions asked in the research instrument. Perhaps only slightly less clear is the fact that the research instrument questions should be appropriate for the population being studied. Nevertheless, many thesis writers seem to feel that they must ask a specific number of questions, and they sometimes ask questions that have no direct relevance to the population being studied or to the research question. Some unnecessary questions fall into the category of being considered "personal" or "confidential" by most people. There is no justification for such questions when they cannot be directly related to the research question.

One student, for example, asked how many times the questionnaire respondent had been divorced or widowed. Her thesis related to travel agency rebating. When asked why this rather unusual and definitely personal question was included on her questionnaire, she responded that there was room on the page, it helped to fill the page, and she thought it would be interesting information for her to have. None of these constitute valid reasons for including such a question. "More" is not necessarily "better" when it comes to research instrument questions.

The more questions you ask, the less likely the respondent will be to answer all your questions. Analyze each question. Ask yourself how it relates to the research question, the hypotheses, the problems, and the subproblems. If the question does not have a direct relationship to some aspect of your thesis, the question should be eliminated. Even if there is a direct relationship, you may need to reword the question several times to make certain that it will elicit the type of response you need. Make the questions clear and concise; they need to be easily understood by the reader.

In preparing the questionnaire, you should keep the population in mind. Questions should be appropriate for the target population. For example, if you wish to identify average tip levels by surveying wait staff, you should not ask questions that only restaurant managers would be able to answer. At the same time, it might not be appropriate to ask restaurant managers questions relating to correlations between client image and average tip. They might know the answer, but the logical target group would be those who deal directly with tips; that is, the wait staff.

Preliminary Research Instrument Development Techniques— Note Cards of Questions

The body of the research instrument is usually made up of questions. The questions should be drafted on note cards, using a pencil so that changes can easily be made. As noted earlier, the more clear and precise the question is, the greater the likelihood of getting the type of response desired. It is usually best to start by going back to the research question itself. Make a list of questions that are closely tied to the research question and that consist of subproblems or subsets of it.

Next, go through the literature review (Chapter Two) and the introductory sections (Chapter One). As you review these chapters, questions will present themselves; write them down on note cards. Throughout the development of Chapters One through Three, you should keep in mind that the research instrument will be key to the development of a good thesis; the research questions should be considered at all times.

It is often beneficial to discuss potential research instrument questions with others. Get together with a small group of students and analyze each person's research question in turn, coming up with questions that relate to each research question. Analyze each of the questions to determine whether or not it would elicit a beneficial response. Go through this process two or three times with different groups, and compare the results.

At this stage, quality is not a vital factor. Any question that seems appropriate for the thesis should be jotted down on a note card and filed away by key word or concept.

In addition to this ongoing question development effort, set aside a specific time to study the research question, hypotheses, problems, and subproblems. Develop questions that will elicit responses that provide information about or answers to the research question, hypotheses, problems, and subproblems. By sitting down and developing questions in two or three intense sessions separated by a week or more, and not looking at the questions developed in previous sessions, you can come up with a large number of potential research instrument questions. Then, during the step of selecting and refining questions, you should have little difficulty in coming up with a reasonable number of high-quality research instrument questions that will ultimately provide data that will allow you to respond to the subproblems and the problems, reach conclusions relating to the hypotheses, and answer the thesis research question.

Preliminary Research Instrument Development Techniques— Interview Sampling

Interview sampling is a time-honored approach in developing a questionnaire. This process involves several steps: (1) Planning—determine what specific target audience will be contacted. (2) Identify when and how the interviews will be conducted. (3) Prepare a list of the questions you will ask. (4) Identify how interview responses will be recorded (usually by audiotape); if audiotaping or videotaping, prepare appropriate permission forms. (5) Document the process in written form and review it with your instructor. Make any changes your instructor advises, and develop an agreed-upon (by instructor and researcher) contact and interviewing process. (6) Contact the individuals you plan to interview and schedule appointments with them. (7) Conduct the interviews. (8) Transcribe the interviews and develop research instrument questions from them.

The Document Review/Revision Process

Each of these steps requires work. For many students, the first five steps—thinking through each aspect of the interviewing process, documenting it, and getting the process approved by the instructor—are the hardest. This process can take some time, so you should develop a rough draft of the procedure early in the academic term, review the draft two or three times (leaving two or three days between each review), and make any necessary revisions. Set up an appointment with your instructor for as early as possible after the final review, and (if the instructor agrees), record the conversation. After each review with your instructor, transcribe the recordings, identify the changes necessary, and make them. At your next meeting, provide your instructor with a list of the recommended changes and show the instructor the changes you have made. During each meeting with your instructor, repeat the process. By doing this, it will be possible to develop a procedure that is fully agreed-upon, and you will be able to move forward rapidly with the interviewing process.

Naturally, students would like to have all problems identified when the first draft is handed in. However, professors review a large number of theses; they do not always remember the changes they recommend, and sometimes they miss noting changes that are needed during the first review but catch them during a second or third review. This is especially true if your English language usage is poor. The instructor may not be able to concentrate on the concepts of the paper because of the language errors.

This can frustrate students. Do not be overly concerned. Most professors are very much aware of the likelihood of it happening, and getting irritated because your professor did not raise some point during your first meeting does nothing to overcome the problem that exists in your thesis. By recording conversations with professors, listing recommendations for changes from those conversations, reviewing them, and recording any additional changes needed the next time around, it is usually possible to obtain final approval from the professor within three drafts. As you and your instructor become more comfortable with this procedure, it is sometimes possible to reduce the number of reviews to two before a mutually agreed-upon document has been developed.

Geographical Sampling Size

The first step in developing the interview sampling is to determine exactly what target audience will be contacted. You may be tempted to limit your sampling to a more narrow or geographically defined area. Better samplings, however, will reduce the potential generalizability problem. You should sample the entire universe of those who will be surveyed with the research instrument, if possible. By working with a sampling of a full target audience, interview sampling has a better chance of reflecting the opinions and viewpoints of a representative group of the total population.

Phone or Personal Visit Sampling

The next step is to identify when and how the sampling will be undertaken. You can conduct the interviews by phone or in person. Obviously, if a large population is used (even for sampling purposes), personal interviews will be prohibitively expensive. If you conduct telephone interviews, you will need to obtain permission (from the individual being interviewed) for the phone interview to be audiotaped. An inexpensive telephone transmitter can be purchased for recording directly from the phone. These can be obtained from electronic discount stores, usually for less than 10 dollars. Ask the person on the phone if they will allow recording, and if they allow it, connect the recording device. Ask them again, this time recording their permission. This saves considerable time in obtaining written authorizations.

Sample Size

The sampling can be as large or as small as you want or can afford. It is usually conducted on a percentage basis, so that you may state that x percentage of all expected respondents were surveyed in the initial interview sampling. This should provide you with anywhere from 50 to several hundred interview samples.

The next step is to prepare a list of the questions that you will ask. Whatever process you follow, you need to develop questions that will help you construct research instrument questions. Time spent now in developing good questions is time saved later.

Refining Final Research Instrument Questions Based on Responses from the Sampling

The last step is the transcription of pertinent aspects of the interviews. The goal is to further refine questions on your final research instrument. Some people are selective regarding the transcription of interviews, transcribing only those parts of the interviews that they feel will be beneficial in developing better research instrument questions. If you elect to follow this process, it is better to conduct the transcription yourself, rather than have a secretary or an assistant do it. You are in the best position to make value judgements as to what is pertinent to your thesis; you can make immediate decisions as to whether or not the material being listened to should be transcribed.

Alternatively, entire interviews can be transcribed, set aside, and reviewed later. Although you will have more to listen to, you can base decisions on the total transcription, rather than a part of it. Whatever process you use, you must transcribe some or all of the interviews and review the transcriptions, pulling out potential refinements of or additions to your research instrument questions.

The Delphi Approach

A related approach to developing and refining research instrument questions is the Delphi approach. One version of the Delphi approach is to gather together several small groups of potential questionnaire respondents and ask each group the same set of questions, recording and taking notes throughout. This is usually done in several cities. You guide the discussion and lead the experts through the process of identifying pertinent questions for the research instrument. The results of each Delphi group are compared to one another, and those outcomes that appear to be most strongly reinforced (for example, patterns appearing in each group discussion) are compared to research instrument questions developed through more traditional approaches. The outcome will usually be two or more sets of similar questions. The Delphi-developed research questions provide a vehicle for refining or adding to previously designed questions. Some people follow up this approach by sending the results to the participants in each Delphi group. They are asked if they agree with the results, and, if they do not agree, to identify what the problems are.

This approach works well when there are groups of experts in several closely located cities. However, if you must travel all over the country, it can be impractical. In the hospitality industry, this approach has been used with groups of restaurant managers in various cities, hotel marketing executives in several major cities that are located near one another, and so on.

Some people solve the distance problem by attending one or more national conventions, at which they conduct small group sessions. Most national associations in the hotel, restaurant, meeting, and travel industries cooperate with (and often assist) students who conduct group interviews for research purposes during their national conventions.

Writing the First Draft of the Research Instrument

The first draft of the research instrument is taken from the questions that you developed earlier and put on note cards. Review similar questions, deleting or rewording questions as necessary. Where cross-checks (the same question worded differently in a different part of the questionnaire to make sure the respondent is answering consistently) are needed, reworded questions will need to be prepared and distributed at appropriate points throughout the questionnaire. Refine the note card questions using the approaches discussed earlier in this chapter. Simplify the wording of the questions wherever possible.

Of crucial importance is tieing the research instrument questions to the thesis research question. Some research instrument questions may be related to the statistical treatments contemplated for the study. Others should be related directly to hypotheses, problems, and subproblems. Prepare a plan for visual data displays. This is an integral part of Chapter Three of the thesis; it is discussed in detail in Chapter 9 of this book.

Writing the Cover Letter

The cover letter to the research instrument needs to be brief and to the point. (For examples of the cover letter and a sample questionnaire, see Figures 7.1–7.3.) It also needs to establish your credibility and the credibility of the original research project. A letter that is long or confusing may not be read, and a letter that does not establish credibility may not motivate the reader to complete the questionnaire. You must write a cover letter that will get the reader to take the action desired: respond to the questionaire accurately and completely. Unless this is done by a significant number of the recipients of the questionnaire, the data needed to complete Chapters Four and Five of the thesis will not be available, and you will have to take actions to overcome the lack of response. These actions are expensive and time-consuming.

The cover letter needs to be brief, concise, and to the point, but it also needs to be complete. It contains the following four points: (1) it identifies the researcher; (2) it addresses confidentiality; (3) it establishes that response is essential for the success of the research; and (4) it establishes that participating in the study is in the respondent's interest because of the benefits the results will provide.

Most cover letters consist of no more than two paragraphs. In the first paragraph you introduce yourself, the academic institution for which the thesis project is being undertaken, the subject of study, and the thesis topic. In the second paragraph, the reader is asked to respond to the questionnaire, is usually offered a synopsis of the outcomes, and is provided with student contact information. Benefits to the industry that can be expected as a result of the thesis research (and benefits to the potential respondent) are briefly set out. If data will be kept confidential or if the study is blind (data cannot be tracked back to any specific respondent), this is noted, and the steps taken to ensure the confidentiality of respondents are described. Finally, in either the second paragraph or a third paragraph specifically oriented to it, the reader is thanked in advance for completing the research instrument and sending it back. Usually, a deadline by which the completed research instrument is needed is provided here as well.

**THE
GEORGE
WASHINGTON
UNIVERSITY**

Washington, D.C. 20052 / Department of Educational Leadership / (202) 994-6940

February 1, 1988

Dear Travel and Tourism Program Chair/Director:

I am conducting a nationwide study of community college based
(two-year) travel and tourism programs. This study is under the
auspices of the School of Education and Human Development, The
George Washington University. The results will provide much
needed information about the operation of travel and tourism
programs in community colleges.

The final phase of this study is enclosed herein in the form of a
brief questionnaire which will require only five minutes of your
time to complete. Please enclose the completed questionnaire in
the self-addressed envelope which has been provided for your
convenience.

Since this is among the pioneer studies of community college
based tourism programs I especially welcome your participation
and shall be happy to share the results with you upon its
conclusion.

Your cooperation in this nationwide study is very much
appreciated. The results will be forwarded to you as soon as
possible.

Sincerely yours,

Stuart A. Schulman
c/o Dr. Joseph A. Greenberg
School of Education and Human Development
The George Washington University
2201 G Street, NW
Washington, DC 20052

Figure 7.1
*Courtesy of
Dr. Stuart A.
Schulman*

Metropolitan ▲ State College of Denver

**Department of Hospitality, Meeting
and Travel Administration**

January 05, 1993

Ms. Anne Grecko
Meeting Planner
Klavern Hospital Supplies
918 W. Jewell
Lakewood, Texas 98762

Dear Ms. Grecko;

Each year senior students enrolled with the Hospitality,
Meeting, and Travel Administration department at Metropolitan
State College in Denver conduct research projects to meet
graduation requirements. The enclosed questionnaire is designed
to compare what services meeting planners expect from
university-based meeting centers when holding a meeting and what
services university-based meeting centers are providing for
meeting planners and their attendees.

It would be greatly appreciated if you would take this
opportunity to advise us of the services you would like for your
meetings when they are held at university-based meeting centers.
Your answers will then be compared to the questionnaires
received from university-based meeting center directors listing
the services they currently provide.

Please use the enclosed envelope to return your answers. Having
the completed questionnaire returned by March 05, 1993 will
allow enough time to evaluate the results of the study. Thank
you for your time and cooperation in completing this
questionnaire.

Sincerely;

Mary A. Mincer
Student, MSCD

Enc.

Campus Box 60
P.O. Box 173362
Denver, Colorado 80217-3362
Office: (303)556-3152

Figure 7.2
*Modified
MSCD HMTA
Thesis
Component. Re-
produced with
permission.*

THE
GEORGE
WASHINGTON
UNIVERSITY

Washington, D.C. 20052 / Department of Educational Leadership / (202) 994-6940

A STUDY OF INSTITUTIONAL LINKAGE:
TRAVEL & TOURISM EDUCATION AT COMMUNITY COLLEGES IN THE UNITED STATES

A.   **GENERAL INFORMATION**

1.   The term "linkage," as used in this study, refers to the institutional housing or placement of a travel and tourism program within the structure of the community college.

2.   Community College, as used in this study includes any institution accredited to award the Associate degree as its highest degree. This includes comprehensive two-year colleges as well as many technical institutes both public and private.

3.   Travel & Tourism as used in this study is an interactive, multi-component and professional learning system with open architecture that relates individual and group travel elements with destination, transportation, hospitality and communication networks.

B.   **DIRECTIONS**

As a community-junior college travel and tourism program chair/program director, you are asked to respond to each item within the various areas of inquiry presented regarding linkage satisfaction. Please read each statement listed below and respond as follows:

Part A: Relates to situational variables. Please circle the most appropriate response. If none is appropriate, please fill in the blank space.

Part B: Relates to five perceived dimensions of linkage satisfaction. Please circle the number which best describes your level of satisfaction in each area.

The survey data is being collected, tabulated, and analyzed under the auspices of the George Washington University. Your answers to this questionnaire will be held in the utmost confidence by the George Washington University. You need not identify yourself on the questionnaire or on the return address envelope.

Thank you for your interest and returning the questionnaire no later than Friday, February 26, 1988.

Return in the envelope provided by February 26, 1988
or send to:

Mr. Stuart A. Schulman
c/o Dr. Joseph A. Greenberg
School of Education and Human Development
The George Washington University
2201 G Street, NW
Washington, DC   20052

Figure 7.3
*Courtesy of
Dr. Stuart A.
Schulman*

PART A   SITUATIONAL VARIABLES

INSTRUCTIONS: Please circle the most appropriate response - if
                none is appropriate, please complete the indicated
                blank space.

PERSONAL PROFILE

1. Sex: A. Male   B. Female

2. Age: A. 21-35   B. 36-45   C. 46-55   D. 56-65

3. Please circle the item that most accurately describes your
    present level of academic achievement:

            A. I presently hold a Doctorate in travel and tourism.

            B. I presently hold a Doctorate in a related field.

            C. I presently hold a Doctorate in another field.

            D. I am presently working on my Doctorate.

            E. I have not begun Doctoral studies.

4. Do you have professional travel industry experience:

            A. Yes   B. No

    5. If Yes, the length of your professional experience is:

            A. 0-3 years   B. 4-6 years   C. 7-9 years   D. other_____

6. Do you participate in the following activities:

    6. Professional consulting   A. Yes   B. No

    7. Writing professional articles
        and texts   A. Yes   B. No

    8. Speaking at professional seminars
        and meetings   A. Yes   B. No

    9. Attending professional seminars
        and meetings   A. Yes   B. No

PROFESSIONAL PROFILE

10. Present Title:

            A. Program Chair   B. Program Director

            C. Program Administrator C. other_____

Figure 7.3
(continued)

A good cover letter can accomplish all these tasks in approximately half a page. Draft the letter, set it aside, and go back to it one or more times. Revise as necessary until the letter is in the format desired by you and your instructor.

Summary

The questionnaire is the foundation for original research. In developing the questionnaire, it is important to tie the population and the research question to the research instrument (the questionnaire), and it is important to avoid personal or confidential questions; ask questions that will allow you to reach conclusions relating to the subproblems, the problems, the hypotheses, and the research question of the thesis. The questionnaire should not be so long that it will not be answered, but it needs to be complete.

Developing questions that meet the needs of the thesis is a challenge. Questions are drafted on note cards, based on a thorough review of the research question, the literature review, and all sections of Chapter One. Students can review one another's questions, making suggestions, or they can get together in groups to pose questions for the research instruments being developed by each member of the group. Most people find that if they set aside a specific time to develop questions, a review of the research question, hypotheses, problems, and subproblems will lead them to appropriate questions for the research instrument.

In developing the research instrument, you can use an interview sampling process. The first step is to plan the entire interview sampling process. Next, contact individuals and interview them. Transcribe the interviews and extract data that will add to or polish the research instrument.

Obtaining the approval of your professor is necessary. This approval usually relates to the plan or the process, but your instructor may require each written portion of the thesis (and the processor instruments used in developing the thesis) to be approved. A process of submitting documentation, meeting with the professor to review the documentation, recording the professor's comments, making changes, documenting the changes, and going back to the professor with a list of documented changes (showing the professor where the changes have been made), allows you to reduce the number of alterations to the thesis, thesis planning process, research instrument, and so on. It also helps you reduce the number of meetings required with your professor.

In considering the sampling, you must determine the geographical size that will be sampled, and determine whether the sampling will be taken by phone or in person. There are pros and cons to each.

Refining the final research instrument questions based on the responses from the sampling requires you to review the sampling responses and identify new questions that should be adopted for the research instrument. Identifying refinements to existing questions that will help to improve the draft research instrument is also beneficial.

Small group meetings are another approach for developing and refining research instrument questions. Small groups of industry experts pose and discuss potential questions. The proceedings are recorded and transcribed. The transcription provides a list of research questions that can be compared to the research questions developed from more traditional approaches. By comparing questions and question wording, it is possible to further refine the research instrument.

Writing the first draft of the research instrument starts with a transcription of questions from the note cards. These should have been grouped into categories of questions. Where response consistency cross-checks are desired, reworded questions should be prepared for placement in various locations throughout the questionnaire.

Next, questions are compared to the question lists developed through the sampling approach and the small group meeting approach. The questionnaire is refined in this manner. Research instrument questions are correlated with major thesis contents (such as the hypotheses, the problems, the subproblems, and the research question). Finally, the research questions are developed into a plan for visual data displays, which will be used in Chapters Three and Four.

The research instrument is of little value without a cover letter. The cover letter needs to be concise and credible. It should offer a synopsis of the study's outcomes to the person who is asked to complete the questionnaire, it should identify how the study will contribute to the industry, and it should motivate the recipient to complete the questionnaire and send it back on time.

Discussion Questions

These questions may be discussed by two or more students outside of class, or they may be discussed during class for a more wide-ranging discussion.

1. On what are most theses written at the bachelor's degree level in programs relating to the hospitality industry founded, and what are they often called?

2. What should the research instrument cover letter offer, and what should it identify?

3. Explain the following statement: "The research questionnaire can be considered to be one foundation for the concept of the term *original*."

4. Why is the questionnaire sometimes considered a "reaction survey?"

5. What four points should be contained in the research instrument cover letter?

6. If a direct relationship does not exist between a research instrument question and one or more of the subproblems, problems, hypotheses, or the research question, should this question be eliminated from the questionnaire? Explain.

7. What is the first step in developing the research instrument interview sampling process?

8. What time-honored approach to developing research questions was discussed in this chapter?

9. For what is the reader of the research instrument cover letter thanked in advance?

10. How should you obtain permission to record a telephone interview?

Role Play Exercises

Two students may participate in these role play exercises either outside of class or as in-class exercises. One plays the role of the first student and the other plays the role of the second student. Read the scripts and then pick up the conversations in your own words.

1. **FIRST STUDENT:** I know my English language isn't too good and that the professor has to wade through a lot of grammatical errors and spelling mistakes, but I don't see why the professor can't tell me everything that is wrong with a draft the first time it is reviewed.

   SECOND STUDENT: I know it is frustrating to obtain a draft with change recommendations, make the recommendations, hand in a revised draft, and get corrections back from the professor on material on which there were no corrections made the first time around. This makes you think either the professor did not read the material the first time or the professor has become a lot more picky over a few weeks. However, in defense of our professor, let me point out that...

Continue on Your Own

2. FIRST STUDENT: I started doing telephone interviews yesterday and I felt like a fool asking industry executives if I could interview them on the phone and then asking them the same question after starting to tape record. I don't see what a big deal it is having to get their permission to record before starting the recording.

    SECOND STUDENT: Getting the permission to record and having it on file through the means of a tape recording gives you protection.

    FIRST STUDENT: I think I understand that, but why shouldn't I just go ahead and record each phone conversation. If the person says they won't give permission, I can simply erase the minute or so of conversation I have with them up to that time. For those who agree to let me tape record, it will eliminate having to go back, reconnect the recorder to the phone, and most important, it will eliminate the need to ask the person I'm speaking with for permission to record two times in the space of maybe five minutes.

    SECOND STUDENT: That would appear on the surface to be the best approach. It is certainly the easiest approach. However...

    Continue on Your Own

3. FIRST STUDENT: I really don't see why I should have to do a cover letter for the questionnaire. Why don't I just put a couple of lines of instructions at the top of the questionnaire and send it out all by itself?

    SECOND STUDENT: That would be easier and it would possibly save postage. Nevertheless...

    Continue on Your Own

7.1. The First Draft of the Cover Letter

Review the information in this chapter about writing a research instrument cover letter. Based on this review, prepare a first draft of the cover letter that will accompany your questionnaire. Type your name at the top of the cover letter draft.

To your completed cover letter draft, attach an Instructor Comment Sheet. Make sure the Instructor Comment Sheet has the Assignment section filled in and that it has your name on it. Place the cover letter draft and the Instructor Comment Sheet into an 8.5" × 11" manila envelope with a clasp flap with your name typed on the envelope. If your instructor requests it, include a blank, top-quality audiotape (30 minutes long) with your name printed on it, so that your professor may give you feedback.

7.2. Research Instrument Item Analysis Correlating Individual Research Instrument Questions with Each Subproblem and Each Hypothesis

Type your name at the top of the next two pages. In the spaces provided, type (double-spaced) the information called for. This will be your correlation of research instrument questions with the subproblems and hypotheses you have selected for your research question and for your thesis. You may need more pages than those provided. If so, photocopy additional blank pages as needed, and attach the photocopies to the pages provided.

Before preparing this assignment to hand in, review the information in this chapter, previous chapters, and your research relating to the development of research questions, subproblems, and hypotheses, and the correlation of research instrument questions to the subproblems and hypotheses. To the completed correlations, attach an Instructor Comment Sheet. Make sure the Instructor Comment Sheet has the Assignment section filled in and that it has your name on it. Place the assignment sheets (and any photocopies) and the Instructor Comment Sheet into an 8.5" × 11" manila envelope with a clasp flap with your name typed on the front of the envelope. If your instructor requests it, include a blank, top-quality audiotape (30 minutes long) with your name on it, so that your professor may give you feedback.

Research Instrument Questions Correlated with Subproblems and Hypotheses

Subproblem number one: _____

_____

    Question number _____: _____

    _____

    Question number _____: _____

    _____

    Question number _____: _____

    _____

Subproblem number two: _____

_____

    Question number _____: _____

    _____

    Question number _____: _____

    _____

    Question number _____: _____

    _____

Subproblem number three: _____

_____

    Question number _____: _____

    _____

    Question number _____: _____

    _____

    Question number _____: _____

    _____

Hypothesis number one: _____
_____

    Question number _____: _____
    _____

    Question number _____: _____
    _____

    Question number _____: _____
    _____

Hypothesis number two: _____
_____

    Question number _____: _____
    _____

    Question number _____: _____
    _____

    Question number _____: _____
    _____

Hypothesis number three: _____
_____

    Question number _____: _____
    _____

    Question number _____: _____
    _____

    Question number _____: _____
    _____

7.3. Second Draft of Chapter One

Review the following: (1) information in this chapter that relates to Chapter One of the thesis; (2) information in all previous chapters regarding the writing of Chapter One; (3) your first draft of Chapter One; and (4) your instructor's comments regarding your first draft of Chapter One. Based on these, prepare a second draft of Chapter One. Be sure that it includes all required components and any optional components you wish to include. Type your name at the top of each page.

To your completed second draft of Chapter One, attach an Instructor Comment Sheet. Make sure the Instructor Comment Sheet has the Assignment section filled in and that it has your name on it. Place the second draft of Chapter One and the Instructor Comment Sheet into an 8.5" × 11" manila envelope with a clasp flap with your name typed on the envelope. If your instructor requests it, include a blank, top-quality audiotape (30 minutes long) with your name printed on it, so that your professor may give you feedback.

Chapter Three—
The Foundation

Upon completion of this chapter, you will be able to:

1. Describe the target population from which original data in the form of question-naire responses will be sought.

2. List six criteria for the admissibility of data.

3. Write five validity criteria to be met by either the sample to be considered or the re-search instrument to be used in your thesis.

4. Compare six types of validity and describe how each type applies to your thesis.

Introduction

Chapter Three is the foundation of the original research paper. This chapter sets out the exact parameters of how the research will be conducted. It ties the research process to the research question, the hypotheses, the problems, the subproblems, and each of the research instrument questions. It identifies the statistical treatments that will be given to the analyses of each body of data and explains why these statistical analyses have been selected. This chapter identifies how the results of the statistical analyses will be presented (usually in chart, graph, or figure format) and why this presentation has been selected.

Chapter Three further sets out the parameters of the study by providing a detailed description of the population and reasons why this population has been selected. It identifies techniques and approaches used to establish research validity and reliability.

Chapter Three identifies the mechanics that will be followed. It explains how and when the mailings were conducted, and follow-up procedures in the event that an insufficient number of responses to the first mailing were received. It presents a timetable for the mailing and for one or more follow-up mailings. If the research instrument or envelopes are to be coded, it explains how and why. Chapter Three provides an explanation of the entire research process, and it provides the reasons for the selection of various process options.

In this chapter, only some of the sections of Chapter Three will be discussed and explained. A reintroduction to the concepts of primary and secondary data will be provided, with an explanation of how to tie primary and secondary data together, and how this tie-in is explained in Chapter Three. This chapter also explains why some data discovered through the research process may not be admissible for consideration. It suggests parameters for admissibility of data and shows how these parameters are presented in Chapter Three.

Primary and Secondary Data

As discussed in Chapters 1, 2, and 6 of this book, data are of two types: primary and secondary. Chapter Two, the review of related literature, is where pertinent secondary data are identified and discussed. This is information taken from the literature. Because it is taken from publications, it is considered secondary data.

Primary data are data that were obtained as a result of your research effort, gathered through the data instrument or questionnaire. It is not only the raw data on the questionnaire response form; it is also the analysis of that data and the grouping of statistical information from the responses.

In Chapter Two of the original thesis, secondary data are presented and discussed. In Chapter Three, the relationship between secondary and primary data is reviewed. This sets the parameters for all aspects of the study. In Chapter Four, the original data obtained is identified, set out, displayed in chart, graph, table, or figure formats, and reviewed. In Chapter Five, the secondary and primary data are discussed and interpreted as the combination of data relates to the original research question.

Chapter Three discusses the projected relationship between primary and secondary data. You should consider the results found in the review of the literature and should identify how those results affect the research question and the data that you expect to obtain from the research questionnaire. These relationships should be identified and fully explored in Chapter Three. Each relationship will warrant a paragraph, and often it will be surrounded by an introductory paragraph and a concluding paragraph (providing analyses of the expected relationships between the primary and the secondary data).

Criteria for the Admissibility of Data

You should be selective in choosing the data that you will use in your study. Secondary data is screened for pertinency to the research question when writing Chapter Two. This screening process is fairly simple and is related strictly to your evaluation of how relevant the data are to your study. Data that appear to be skewed should have the skew probability noted when presenting the data, and, in Chapter Five, secondary data skew probabilities should be explained and justified (if possible).

Data considered in Chapter Three of the thesis relate to the original data (obtained as a result of the questionnaire), which will be either accepted or rejected. It is expected that you will identify reasons for the rejection of data and will, in fact, reject data that fall into the classifications identified as unacceptable.

The reasons for rejection relate to the quality of the data received and the data-gathering process. Just because a researcher does not "like" the response is insufficient reason to reject the data. Neither is the receipt of data that conflict with the data received from other respondents. Reasons for rejecting data can vary from one research study to the next. For example, some researchers feel—with justification—that unless the questionnaire is entirely completed, the partial responses should be rejected. In other words, if the respondent selectively answers questions, a true picture may not be obtained; the data from that questionnaire may be biased or incomplete.

Another reason for the rejection of data is that the data may have been provided by an unqualified person. For example, if your study relates to hotel marketing budgets, you might decide that responses from hotel marketing executives, hotel chief executive officers, and hotel financial executives are acceptable, but a response from the head housekeeper is unacceptable.

There are many reasons why you might consider data to be unacceptable. These reasons should be considered in advance and should be detailed in this section of Chapter Three.

Validity

There are two major criteria with which measurements used in the thesis are evaluated: validity and reliability (Noll, 1965, p. 77). Validity considers what is measured or evaluated, and asks if you are actually measuring what you say you are measuring in your thesis. The first place where validity is considered is the research question itself.

A major validity consideration applying to the research question asks, "Can you realistically expect to answer the research question as it is stated with the research instrument being used?" For example, consider the following research question: "What experience, training, and background are necessary to obtain an in-flight services attendant (flight attendant) position with an American air carrier?" Although this research question may or may not be a good one, and it certainly has some potential for concern, when you consider the research instrument that the student sent to air carrier in-flight services recruiters, you need to ask several questions regarding validity. Some of these questions relate to the concept of "face validity" (does the research instrument measure what it is supposed to measure?) (Leedy, 1985, p. 25). One of these questions would be: "Will this research instrument determine what experience, background, and training are necessary to obtain an in-flight services position?" If the instrument is sent to in-flight services recruiters working with all U.S.-based air carriers, those aspects of the research question that relate to geographic parameters may not need to be considered further. However, the key face-validity question is: "Does the instrument actually do what it is expected to do—that is, will it provide the data needed to determine what experience, training, and background are necessary to obtain an in-flight services position?" This is a value judgment on your part, but it also will be a value judgment made by your professor, and by anyone else who may read the study. If the conclusion is that the research instrument does not do this, then it does not have the validity necessary to provide you with the data needed to complete the thesis.

A second question relating to face validity concerns the sample being considered. Is the sample representative of the behavior or trait being measured? (Leedy, 1985, p. 25.) If the research instrument is sent to all U.S.-based air carrier in-flight services recruiters, you might feel that the survey population is sufficiently broad. However, if you received responses from a limited number of in-flight services recruiters, and especially if those responses were from a small, identifiable segment of U.S.-based air carriers, you would have to question the face validity of the study results. For example, if only air carriers based in California responded, and the study purported to identify the background, experience, and training necessary to obtain an in-flight services position with any or all American air carriers, you would have to conclude that the research results were invalid.

In addition to face validity, there are at least five other types of validity that you should consider. These include construct validity, content validity, criterion validity, and internal and external validity. The last two have to do with the interpretation of data more than the compilation of data. Internal validity relates to the avoidance of conclusion bias based on data; external validity relates to the avoidance of generalizations from too small or too narrow a sample (Leedy, p. 25). "A study has internal validity if the outcome of the study is a function of the program or approach being tested rather than the result of other causes not systematically dealt with in the study," whereas "a study has external validity if the results obtained would apply in the real world to other similar approaches" (Tuckman, 1972, p. 4).

Make sure your study maintains internal and external validity. Guard against the problems of conclusion bias and generalizing from too small or too narrow a sample. If you approach your research with predetermined conclusions, it is easy to find that the interpreted results from the data may be too broad or biased. In the case of the research question considered earlier, if the responses were received only from California-based air carriers, and you interpreted the results to apply to all U.S. air carriers, you have violated external validity; you generalized from too narrow a base of information. You might go into the study believing that any predetermined set of circumstances met by applicants might provide them with an advantage in obtaining employment in in-flight services and, with that bias in mind, interpret the results to appear to justify the predetermined bias. Be careful to avoid this.

Construct validity, sometimes called "logical validity" (Noll, 1965, p. 81), has to do with accurately measuring concepts (Leedy, 1985, p. 25). The ability to accurately measure a concept is especially difficult, because concepts cannot be directly observed. Concept validity is concerned with the ability to measure the concept to some degree of agreed-upon accuracy. Consider this research question: "Are extroverts more successful than introverts as front desk personnel in a downtown hotel?" You must define the words "extrovert" and "introvert." After defining the terms, you must determine some degree of validity in measuring whether a given individual is an introvert or an extrovert. The ability to accurately do this relates to establishing construct validation or validity.

There are a number of tests that purport to be able to differentiate concepts. However, guard against creating impractical situations when setting up construct validity tests. For example, it is unlikely that you are going to be able to get front desk people from throughout the United States to take personality inventory tests in order to determine whether they are introverts or extroverts. Even if a significant number of front desk personnel were willing to take such tests, administering them in such a way that the consistency of the tests would be assured would probably be impractical.

Criterion validity employs a check in areas where there may be concern about the accuracy of the first measure. In most studies, the technique used is to ask the same question in two different ways and review the results to determine whether or not the respondent answered in a consistent manner. Usually, if the respondent answered the question at a point early in the questionnaire in the same way as a variation of that question later in the questionnaire, criterion validity is confirmed. However, if the response were substantially different, accuracy is not verified through the cross-check. For that particular questionnaire item, criterion validity should be questioned.

Content validity is similar to face validity. It "is the accuracy with which an instrument measures the factors or situations under study" (Leedy, 1985, p. 25). In other words, "content validity estimates are essentially systematic, but subjective, evaluations of the appropriateness of the measuring instrument for the task at hand" (Tull & Hawkins, 1984, p. 244). Tull and Hawkins point out that content validity is most often used with multi-item measures, assessing "the representativeness, or sampling adequacy, of the needed items in light of the purpose of the measuring instrument" (p. 244). For example, a questionnaire purporting to measure the public's attitude toward a hotel would not be considered to have content validity if the measuring instrument left out any major attribute such as location, layout, and so on. "Content validation," according to Tull and Hawkins, "is the most common form of validation in applied marketing research" (p. 244).

All facets of validity must be met and maintained before the research instrument can be considered valid to obtain the measurements needed to prove the thesis hypotheses and research questions.

Reliability

Reliability is a measure of accuracy and response consistency. Reliability concerns in the research lie with the accuracy and consistency of the research (Leedy, 1985, p. 26; Noll, 1965, p. 84). In applying reliability measures to the research instrument, the question is: "How accurately and how consistently does this research instrument question measure what it is intended to measure?" Extending the same reasoning to the research instrument as a whole, the question is: "How accurately and how consistently does this research instrument measure what needs to be measured in terms of providing an answer to the research question?"

Accuracy deals with two components. The first is a measure of how well and how consistently the research instrument addresses the research question; the second is how accurately and how consistently the individual questions in the research instrument measure that which must be measured in order to provide an answer to the research question. The first problem is often greater: developing and designing research questions that precisely and completely pertain to the research question. Once this is accomplished, you can turn to the individual questions and assess their reliability.

You can measure reliability by applying statistical and nonstatistical tests to the research instrument and to each of the individual questions. According to Sax, "the reliability of a set of measurements obtained from questionnaires may be determined by using coefficients of stability, equivalence, or internal consistency (homogeneity)" (1968, p. 230). One of the simplest tests is to administer the same questionnaire to a group of respondents twice over a short period of time. The correlation between the scores is the coefficient of stability. If items are poorly constructed, answers may vary simply because the respondent is unsure what the question is asking. But leave little time between administering the tests (no more than a month). The respondent's beliefs, attitudes, and opinions can change over time, resulting in variations unrelated to questionnaire item construction (Sax, 1968, pp. 230–231).

Usually, several reliability tests are administered. According to Tull and Hawkins, there are five approaches you can use to assess reliability. These are: "(1) test-retest reliability (applying the same measure to the same objects a second time); (2) split-sample reliability (dividing the sample into two [or more] random subsamples and testing to see if the variation in each of the items of interest is within the range of sampling error); (3) alternative-forms reliability (measuring the same objects by two instruments that are designed to be as nearly alike as possible); (4) internal-comparison reliability (comparing the responses among the various items on a multiple-item index designed to measure a homogeneous concept); and (5) scorer reliability (comparing the scores assigned the same qualitative material by two or more judges)" (Tull & Hawkins, 1984, p. 241).

Tull and Hawkins state that, "no one approach is best; in fact, several different assessment approaches should generally be used" (p. 241). Most researchers select the two or three reliability tests that will best determine (and ultimately establish) the reliability of their research instrument. The specific reliability tests are discussed in Chapter Three of the thesis, and the procedures for administering these tests are detailed. Your professor may suggest additional or different tests for establishing research instrument reliability.

The Chapter Three Population Description

The Chapter Three population description should be precise. It should identify the exact parameters of the population that will be addressed. If a sampling approach is to be used, it should identify exactly how that sampling will be taken, what percentage will be sampled, and why the sampling decisions made have been made. It is usually better to work with an established population that can be documented. For example, the population might consist of all members of a national association, and the description of that might be those members whose names and addresses have been published in the national directory of that association. This approach allows you to use the parameters and frameworks developed by others in the industry to narrow the population to a reasonable size. Once the population has been determined, the approach used to sample the population is described in detail.

Study the population example in Figure 8.1. Note how the author has selected a population base determined by a national organization recognized in the industry for its standards. Notice also how the author is detailed and specific in describing the quality, accuracy, timeliness, and comprehensiveness of the list. The sampling technique is spelled out, using a third-party expert (Leedy) for the sampling process. The cost and the timely receipt process are specified. Finally, the author spells out why this list was selected, as opposed to other possible lists. All these points need to be made in a well-written "Population" section for Chapter Three of the thesis.

Summary

This chapter deals with the foundation components of Chapter Three of the thesis. It first identifies the purposes of Chapter Three, and it establishes the specific parameters of the thesis. The concepts of primary and secondary data are reviewed, and an explanation of how they are discussed in Chapter Three is addressed.

This chapter concentrates its attention on four specific parts of Chapter Three: (1) the criteria for the admissibility of data; (2) validity; (3) reliability; and (4) the Chapter Three population description.

Much of the chapter is devoted to the consideration of validity. Establishing validity is one of the major problems students encounter in writing theses. Several types of validity are considered and discussed in this chapter: face validity, construct validity, content validity, criterion validity, internal validity, and external validity.

Bibliography

Leedy, Paul D. *Practical Research Planning and Design,* 3rd ed. New York: Macmillan, 1985.

Noll, Victor H. *Introduction to Educational Measurement*, 2nd ed. Boston: Houghton Mifflin, 1965.

Sax, Gilbert. *Empirical Foundations of Educational Research.* Englewood Cliffs, New Jersey: Prentice-Hall, 1968.

Tuckman, Bruce W. *Conducting Educational Research.* New York: Harcourt Brace Jovanovich, 1972.

Tull, Donald S., and Hawkins, Del I. *Marketing Research Measurement and Method.* New York: Macmillan, 1984.

The population will consist of those individuals named as travel agency "qualifiers" on the Airline Reporting Corporation's (ARC) list of approximately 41,000 "appointed" travel agencies in the United States. The list is computer-generated by the Airline Reporting Corporation and is produced on a "demand" basis whenever a list is processed. Usually, there is at least one list purchase processed each day. The list is updated continuously. All travel agencies that are allowed to maintain and sell domestic U.S. airline "standard" ticket stock must be appointed by the Airline Reporting Corporation before they are allowed to receive a supply of ticket stock. One criterion of appointment is for the agency to employ one named and designated agency "qualifier." This person must pass an examination based on the *Airline Reporting Corporation Handbook.*

The ARC list of qualifiers will be generated on peel-off address labels. One out of every 50 names will be used starting with a random number selected through Leedy's dollar bill entry number process (Leedy, 1985, p.#150). This means the total mailing will be to approximately 820 agency qualifiers (one out of every 50 on the ARC list).

The list of qualifiers will be ordered directly from the Airline Reporting Corporation at the address listed in the current issue of the *Airline Reporting Corporation Handbook.* The cost of the list is $0.25 per name on computer-generated peel-off labels. The total cost, therefore, would normally be $10,250. However, the ARC has agreed to run a special selection of one out of every 50 names based on the entry number that the researcher will provide (see former paragraph on entry number selection and see attached letter from ARC agreeing to the special run). The cost for the special run, therefore, will be approximately $205. The exact cost will be quoted by the ARC by phone on the day the order request is mailed. The list order will be processed within 48 business hours of receipt of the request (and of the accompanying check for payment). Distribution can be made by U.S. mail or by Federal Express. No guaranteed delivery time will be quoted for U.S. mail delivery, but the ARC guarantees delivery within 48 business hours after list processing is completed when delivery is made by Federal Express.

Therefore, the Federal Express delivery option will be requested, and payment for same will be made.

The selection of this population over other potential populations was made for the following reasons: (1) It represents the largest and most comprehensive list of U.S.-based travel agencies that meet a specified set of criteria. (2) With the possible exception of the American Society of Travel Agents (ASTA) list of "Direct Members" (which is almost half the size of the ARC list), the ARC qualifier list is the only list of agency "management" persons that is generally agreed to be comprehensive.

BIBLIOGRAPHICAL REFERENCE

Leedy, Paul D. *Practical Research Planning and Design*, 3d ed. New York: Macmillan, 1985.

Figure 8.1 Population example. *Modified MSCD HMTA Thesis Component. Reproduced with permission.*

115

Discussion Questions

These questions may be discussed by two or more students outside of class, or they may be discussed during class for a more wide-ranging discussion.

1. What is Chapter Three called?

2. With what type of population is it usually better to work?

3. What is usually interpreted to be original data?

4. In applying reliability to the research instrument, what two questions are often asked?

5. What should the reader of the thesis encounter for the first time in Chapter Three?

6. The accuracy of the study deals with two components. What are these two components?

7. According to this chapter, what kind of data should you reject?

8. What type of validity determines how accurately the research instrument questions elicit the information needed?

9. There are two major criteria with which measurements used in the thesis are evaluated. What are these two major criteria?

10. In areas where there may be a concern about the accuracy of the first measure, what type of validity calls for a second check?

Role Play Exercises

Two students may participate in these role play exercises either outside of class or as in-class exercises. One plays the role of the first student and the other plays the role of the second student. Read the scripts and then pick up the conversations in your own words.

1. FIRST STUDENT: We sure have to be concerned about a lot of different kinds of validity. I'm going to try to address all of these validity concerns, but I'm not sure that I can. I get the different kinds of validity all mixed up.

   SECOND STUDENT: There are a large number of validity concerns that need to be considered. When I first started working with them, I got them mixed up too. Working with them helps. As you consider an issue, you will begin to train yourself to look at that issue from all validity positions. Sometimes one or more validity concerns will not apply to the issue being considered. However, if you go down the list of each type of validity for each concern you address, you will rapidly understand the differences in types of validity and be able to apply them at an increasingly rapid rate.

   FIRST STUDENT: That makes sense. However, I still don't understand the differences between them.

   SECOND STUDENT: Let me briefly summarize all of them and then I will give you examples of each type. Let's start with content validity. Essentially content validity is concerned with...

Continue on Your Own

2. **FIRST STUDENT:** This concept of setting up criteria for admitting data and rejecting everything else seems ludicrous to me. It seems hard enough to get the raw data in the first place. Why should I then throw out a big chunk of it once I'm able to get it?

SECOND STUDENT: If you don't set up some type of criteria for admitting data, you could have some pretty unreliable data or what might be considered "bad" data, and this could have a number of negative effects.

FIRST STUDENT: I guess that is true, but what kind of criteria should I establish?

SECOND STUDENT: You are the only one who can be the final judge on that issue, but let me give you some guidelines to work with. You can start by...

Continue on Your Own

3. **FIRST STUDENT:** I thought I was confused when I started considering validity, but now I'm faced with the concept of reliability. This really throws me.

SECOND STUDENT: A lot of people have trouble when it comes to the concepts of validity and reliability. Essentially, reliability is...

Continue on Your Own

8.1. Population Source Data Sheet and Population Description

Type your name at the top of the next page. In the space provided, type (double-spaced) the information called for. You may need more room than that provided. If so, continue on one or more pieces of paper. Type your name at the top of each additional sheet and staple all sheets together.

The page after the Population Source Data Sheet is the Draft Population Description. Type your name at the top of this page. In the space provided, type (double-spaced) the information called for. You may need more room than that provided. If so, continue on one or more pieces of paper. Type your name on each sheet, and staple all sheets together before handing them in.

Before preparing this assignment, review the information in this chapter and previous chapters relating to the population to be surveyed for your thesis. To the completed population source data sheet(s) and the completed draft population description, attach an Instructor Comment Sheet. Make sure the Instructor Comment Sheet has the Assignment section filled in and that it has your name on it. Place the completed population source data sheet(s), the completed draft population description sheet(s), and the Instructor Comment Sheet into an 8.5" × 11" manila envelope with a clasp flap with your name typed on the front of the envelope. If your instructor requests it, include a blank, top-quality audiotape (30 minutes long) with your name on it, so that your professor may give you feedback.

Population Source Data Sheet

In the space below, type (double-spaced) a description of the source from which you will receive the list of people or companies to be surveyed in your thesis. Include the name and address of the list company as well as the price of the list. If you are using a directory or another publication, indicate the name and address of the publisher, the cost of the publication, and whether or not you plan to purchase the publication. If you do not plan to purchase the publication, explain how you plan to obtain it. Note the number of names on the list and what geographic or other limitations relate to the list. Use wide margins so that your instructor can make comments.

Draft Population Description

In the space below, type (double-spaced) a brief description of the population on which your thesis will be based. Keep in mind that you should have enough data requests mailed to receive a sufficient number of responses for a valid study. Validity cannot occur without a large number of responses, so make sure that your total population base is substantial. Keep in mind that the thesis needs to be duplicable. In other words, this must be a population that can be reached with ease by another researcher in case a parallel study or a validation study is conducted. Your professor may give you additional guidelines to consider when selecting a population. Leave wide margins so that your professor can make comments.

8.2. Admissibility of Data Criteria and Admissibility of Data Statement

Type your name at the top of the next page. In the spaces provided, type (double-spaced) the information called for.

The page after the Admissibility of Data Criteria Listing is the Admissibility of Data Statement Draft. Type your name at the top of this page. In the space provided, type (double-spaced) the information called for. If you need more room than that provided, continue on one or more pieces of paper. Type your name on each sheet, and staple all sheets together before handing them in.

Before preparing this assignment, review the information in this chapter and from your own research relating to the admissibility of data section of the thesis. To the completed Admissibility of Data Criteria Listing and the completed Admissibility of Data Statement Draft, attach an Instructor Comment Sheet. Make sure the Instructor Comment Sheet has the Assignment section filled in and that it has your name on it. Place the completed Admissibility of Data Criteria Listing, the completed Admissibility of Data Statement Draft, and the Instructor Comment Sheet into an 8.5" × 11" manila envelope with a clasp flap with your name typed on the front of the envelope. If your instructor requests it, include a blank, top-quality audiotape (30 minutes long) with your name on it, so that your professor may give you feedback.

Admissibility of Data Criteria Listing

On the lines below, provide criteria for the admissibility of data for your thesis. Before establishing the criteria for your thesis, review the section in this chapter relating to the admissibility of data. Review any other material relating to this subject that you may have found in your literature review. Be specific about relating these criteria to your thesis.

Criterion number one: _____

_____

Criterion number two: _____

_____

Criterion number three: _____

_____

Criterion number four: _____

_____

Criterion number five: _____

_____

Criterion number six: _____

_____

Admissibility of Data Statement Draft

In the space below, type (double-spaced) an admissibility of data statement for your thesis. Include the criteria established in the Admissibility of Data Criteria Listing. This statement forms a part of Chapter Three, so it should be written in paragraph form. Use wide margins so that your instructor can make appropriate comments.

8.3. Measures of Reliability, Validity Criteria, and Statements of Reliability and Validity

Type your name at the top of the next two pages. In the spaces provided, type (double-spaced) the information called for.

The two pages after the criteria for validity are the Statement of Reliability Draft and the Statement of Validity Draft. Type your name at the top of these pages. In the space provided at the bottom of each page, type (double spaced) the information called for. If you need more room than that provided, continue on one or more pieces of paper. Type your name on each sheet, and staple all sheets together before handing them in.

Before preparing this assignment, review the information in this and previous chapters and from your own research relating to reliability and validity as they apply to theses. To the completed reliability measures, validity criteria, statement of reliability draft, and statement of validity draft, attach an Instructor Comment Sheet. Make sure the Instructor Comment Sheet has the Assignment section filled in and that it has your name on it. Place the completed reliability measures, the completed validity criteria, the completed statement of reliability draft, the completed statement of validity draft, and the Instructor Comment Sheet into an 8.5" × 11" manila envelope with a clasp flap with your name typed on the front of the envelope. If your instructor requests it, include a blank, top-quality audiotape (30 minutes long) with your name on it, so that your professor may give you feedback.

Measures of Reliability

On the lines below, provide three statements, approaches, tests, criteria, or measures of reliability for your thesis. Before you begin, review the section in this chapter relating to reliability, and review any other material relating to reliability that you may have found in your literature review.

Reliability statement, approach, test, criterion, or measure number one:

_____

_____

Reliability statement, approach, test, criterion, or measure number two:

_____

_____

Reliability statement, approach, test, criterion, or measure number three:

_____

_____

Validity Criteria Listing

On the lines below, provide five criteria for the validity of your thesis. Before establishing the validity criteria for your thesis, review the section in this chapter relating to validity, and review any other material relating to validity that you may have found in your literature review.

Criterion number one: _____

_____

_____

Criterion number two: _____

_____

_____

Criterion number three: _____

_____

_____

Criterion number four: _____

_____

_____

Criterion number five: _____

_____

_____

Statement of Reliability Draft

In the space below, type (double-spaced) a draft of the reliability section of Chapter Three of your thesis. Include all aspects and parameters of reliability, and explain how you will ensure that reliability is maintained. Include all three of the statements, approaches, tests, criteria, or measures of reliability that you included in the measures of reliability exercise. Keep in mind that this statement forms a part of Chapter Three, so it should be written in paragraph form. Double-space, and use wide margins so that your instructor can make comments. If you need more room than that provided, continue on one or more pieces of paper. Type your name on each sheet, and staple all sheets together before handing them in.

Statement of Validity Draft

In the space below, type (double-spaced) a draft of the validity section of Chapter Three of your thesis. Remember that there are several types of validity. Address how you will make sure that your thesis maintains each of the following types: face validity, construct validity, content validity, criterion validity, internal validity, and external validity. You should have at least one paragraph relating to each type. Include in your statement of validity all five of the criteria that you included in the validity criteria listing exercise. Keep in mind that this statement forms a part of Chapter Three, so it should be written in paragraph form. Double-space, and use wide margins so that your instructor can make comments. If you need more room than that provided, continue on one or more pieces of paper. Type your name on each sheet, and staple all sheets together before handing them in.

CHAPTER NINE

Chapter Three— The Research Structure

U*pon completion of this chapter, you will be able to:*

1. Write a draft of the research methodologies section of Chapter Three of your thesis.

2. Draft the "Means of Obtaining Data" and "Location of Data" sections for each problem and subproblem of your thesis.

3. Prepare a draft statistical treatment for each research item (by item number) for your thesis.

4. Select an appropriate display (table, figure, chart, or graph) for each statistical treatment applied to each research instrument item of your thesis.

Introduction

The research structure of the thesis is based on research methodologies. In a narrow sense, a research methodology is the treatment that will be applied to the data collected. In a much broader sense, however, research methodology applies to all aspects of data and data interpretation. This includes the population, the research design, the treatment of the data, the instrumentation (the research instrument), and the analysis of the data.

The research structure extends beyond the research methodologies in other ways as well. It addresses the means of obtaining data for each of the problems and subproblems. It identifies the location of the data for each problem and subproblem. It identifies statistical treatment options as they relate to each subproblem, problem, hypothesis, and sometimes (rarely) the research question itself. Identifying treatment options is a task many students shy away from, but it is an integral part of the research structure. In addition, item analyses that will be conducted are identified and discussed, and tables, figures, graphs, and charts appropriate for each item analysis, subproblem treatment, problem treatment, hypothesis treatment, and for each treatment of the research question are identified and discussed. In a very real sense, the research structure becomes the center around which the thesis itself is based.

Research Methodologies

The research methodologies part of the thesis includes sections relating to the population, to research treatments, to the research design, to instrumentation, and to data analysis. The population has already been discussed (see Chapter 8). The treatments explain what will be done in the study.

Many traditional studies include a control group; that is, a part of the population which receives no treatment. For example, if you wanted to determine how chefs learn new recipes best, you would identify a similar population of chefs. These might be chefs with the same amount of experience, with the same amount and type of formal education, and with a background of working in the same type of restaurant. Ideally, they would all be approximately the same age, and as similar as possible in other major ways. One group of chefs (the control group) would be given no instruction, one group could be given a recipe, one group might be given instruction by an expert, and one group might be given a book explaining how to prepare a new food item. Comparisons of the outcomes would be made, and an effort might be made to identify, based on predetermined criteria, which type of learning (or absence of learning) was most effective with chefs. The treatment would be the various approaches used in educating the chefs, including the absence of any education.

The design is similar to the treatment. It is one or more paragraphs that explain what will be done (the treatment) and how it will be done. Identify the control group, the test groups, and the form of manipulation. These points are clearly stated and explained in detail. Dependent and independent variables are also identified and explained.

The instrumentation section identifies precisely what type of research instrument will be used. In most cases it will be a questionnaire of some type. This section of the thesis should not just identify the type of research instrument that will be used, it should also provide reasoning for the selection of the type of research instrument adopted.

The data analysis section of the methodology is frequently the most difficult section for the student who has not yet written a thesis. This is a statistical analysis of the data received. You must identify what statistical analyses will be applied to the data, and you must explain why these analyses have been adopted. Students who have not taken a statistics course often have difficulty with this part of the thesis. If you have difficulty, you can take a course in statistics, review books on statistics, or hire a statistician to tutor you on the thesis statistics. This last option can be expensive and it may be impractical. Keep in mind that you may be required to defend your thesis, and a statistician hired to develop the statistics will not be allowed to accompany you during the defense. Although a hired statistician may do an acceptable job on statistical development, he or she is rarely successful in explaining the statistical applications sufficiently well that you can defend the statistical section of your thesis during an oral defense. It would be best for you to obtain a strong grounding in statistics before developing this part of the thesis.

The Means of Obtaining and the Location of the Data for Each Problem and Subproblem

The research instrument asks a series of questions. The responses constitute the raw data to be used in the thesis. When you consider the means of obtaining data and the location of the data for each problem and subproblem, you are considering which data out of all that constituting the mass of responses (location of data) you will select as the data relate to each problem and subproblem. For example, you might state that research instrument questions number 4, 16, and 19 relate to subproblem number three, and then go on to elaborate. At the same time, you identify the means used in selecting and analyzing the data in order to develop or to "obtain" data for each problem and subproblem.

The location of the data is identified in the thesis by listing the question numbers or the research item numbers. The means of obtaining data is more involved. This is an explanation of how the data was obtained (usually by questionnaire, but sometimes through some other means). It also identifies what the statistical treatment of these research items will be in order to obtain a conclusion relating to the problem or subproblem. This section of the thesis can be (and often should be) lengthy.

Statistical Treatment Options

There are two schools of thought relating to the selection of statistical applications. Purists believe that it is the responsibility of the student researcher to identify the best or most appropriate statistical treatment for each situation and to apply it accordingly. Many academic practitioners, however, believe that this is asking the impossible at the lower levels of academia. Students studying for a baccalaureate degree (including those with a hospitality major) seldom take more than an elementary course in statistics, and this is not sufficient to give them the knowledge or skill needed to wisely select or to broadly apply interpretive statistics. There is no doubt that knowing and being able to apply such applications as how to test hypotheses about a population means, the distribution of z and t analyses of variance, and use of the chi square distribution can be beneficial (and probably will be needed when writing a Ph.D. dissertation). However, practically speaking, students at the baccalaureate level seldom have the statistical knowledge or sophistication to work with these applications. Academic practitioners look at bachelor degree theses as the first step in learning research (with a Ph.D. dissertation or employment in a research position being the last step), and therefore they usually require the use of only descriptive statistics.

Those studying at the bachelor degree level tend to use statistical applications centering around averages and percentages. Many bachelor degree theses include nothing more than the statistical development of a mean, a medium, a mode, or a percentage. Check with your instructor to determine the level of statistical application expected.

Treatment Options for the Data

In addition to the more sophisticated statistical applications, other treatment options for data include ranking data, developing hierarchies, charting the data, and developing a visual (a graph, table, chart, or figure). There are a wide range of additional treatment options as well, but at the bachelor degree level, the options are usually limited to these. As with the more sophisticated statistical applications, it is always wise to discuss non-statistical and less sophisticated statistical treatment options with your professor.

Interpretation of the Data for Each Problem and Subproblem

As Leedy points out, "although facts relative to the problem must be assembled for study and inspection, the extraction of meaning from the accumulated data—what we have called the interpretation of the data—is all important" (1985, p. 166). In Chapter Three, you must identify how data will be interpreted. After developing the research instrument, you send it out, receive responses, report and classify the responses, and apply statistical treatments to the resulting data. At this point, the data must be interpreted.

The first step in the interpretation of the data is to set out or describe the data in several paragraphs, accompanied by appropriate displays (charts, tables, figures, and graphs). Leedy suggests "a basic test for the adequacy of treatment of the data.... The plan for the treatment of the data should be so unequivocal and so specific that any other qualified person seeing only your proposal could carry out your research project without benefit of your presence and by means of your proposal alone." (Leedy, p. 167). Leedy provides eight guidelines for the interpretation of the data. These are as follows: (1) Be systematic in describing the treatment of the data; (2) state the data you need to resolve the problem; (3) state precisely where the data are located; (4) state without equivocation how the data will be secured; (5) state fully and unequivocably precisely how you intend to interpret the data; (6) explain every step in the interpretation of the data; (7) make the research process cyclical; and (8) be sure the data support your conclusions (Leedy, pp. 166–168).

"Make a clear distinction between arraying the data and interpreting the data," states Leedy (p. 168). State why you need the statistical values that you have calculated. Identify how they will extract meaning from the data. Explain why the statistical manipulation you have provided is indispensable to the understanding of the data. Identify the formulas that you used, why you chose those formulas, and where you got them.

Item Analyses

One of the best ways to start the interpretation of the data is to develop analyses of each research question item. Each item in the research questionnaire should relate to some aspect of the research question, the hypotheses, the problems, or the subproblems. Each research question should be given some type of statistical treatment. As with the interpretation of the data for the problems and subproblems, the results of the statistical analysis of each research question item should be presented, and the interpretation of that data should also be presented. Wherever a table, figure, chart, or graph is appropriate, it should be included.

Tables, Figures, Graphs, and Charts

Almost every item analysis should be accompanied by one or more visual displays (tables, figures, graphs, or charts). Research the pros and cons of each type of visual display by reading books relating to them.

In each case, provide the justification for your use of that particular visual display. If you use a figure, provide the reason you used it rather than a table, graph, or chart, and provide the justification for using that figure as opposed to another type of figure. These explanations should be brief, but they must be included.

Basic Review Checks

After Chapter Three has been drafted, check the research structure to make sure that all needed points have been covered and that the flow is smooth and easy to understand. George Allen, in *The Graduate Students' Guide To Theses and Dissertations*, offers these suggested review questions: "1. Did the methodology description follow a logical sequence? 2. Were steps clearly delineated? 3. Were relationships of methodology to the research questions clearly demonstrated? 4. Were controls in the research adequately handled? 5. Were assumptions about uncontrollable factors stated? 6. Were appropriate materials appendixed?" (Allen, 1973, p. 78). Some of Allen's points, such as those dealing with controls, apply to experimental research study designs and therefore may not need to be considered in your thesis, but you should at least review all of Allen's questions for possible relevancy to your thesis.

Summary

Narrowly interpreted, research methodologies, which constitute the central part of the research structure, are the treatments of the data. However, a broad interpretation applies to all aspects of methodology, and includes the population, the research design, the treatment of the data, the instrumentation, and the analysis of the data. This broader interpretation has been the focus of this chapter.

Traditional methodologies start with a division of the population into a control group and one or more experimental groups. However, this is only one type of treatment.

The design is an explanation of the treatments and the reasons for the selection of the treatments. The instrumentation section explains what type of research instrument will be used.

The data analysis section is a statistical analysis of all data. Many students find the statistical analyses to be the most difficult part of Chapter Three. However, the degree of sophistication of statistical application varies depending on the academic level; those writing theses in a B.A. program are usually expected to use only simple (descriptive) forms of statistics.

Most academicians expect you to devote a portion of Chapter Three to a discussion of the means of obtaining the data and the location of the data for each problem and subproblem. To do this, go back to the individual questions in the research instrument and match questions with problems and subproblems. Then select statistical treatments and apply them to the individual questions or groups of data (the outcomes of each or several related questions). Through the statistical applications, you are able to interpret the data for each problem and subproblem. The interpretation needs to be specific (Leedy provides eight interpretation guidelines which are discussed in this chapter). Once each item has been analyzed, visual displays (tables, figures, graphs, or charts) are selected to display the outcome.

The various analyses are grouped together and presented in a sequential flow throughout the chapter, working from each of the subproblems to the problems, from each of the problems to the hypotheses, and from each of the hypotheses to the research question. This is done in a methodical order that presents the entire outcome as a unified whole. The actual presentation of this data is not completed until the research instrument has been completed and returned and Chapter Four is written, but the process of how this is done is the subject of Chapter Three, and the research structure is the focus of Chapter Three.

Bibliography

Allen, George R. *The Graduate Students' Guide To Theses and Dissertations*. San Francisco: Jossey-Bass, 1973.

Leedy, Paul D. *Practical Research Planning and Design,* 3rd ed. New York: Macmillan, 1985.

Discussion Questions

These questions may be discussed by two or more students outside of class, or they may be discussed during class for a more wide-ranging discussion.

1. What do research methodologies constitute in a narrow sense of the term?

2. Visual displays related to item analyses can be one or a combination of as many as four different types. What are these four types?

3. Should the justifications for the use of visual displays be long justifications or short ones?

4. Five subsections are included in the research methodologies section of the thesis. What are these five subsections?

5. According to this chapter, what is one of the best ways to start the interpretation of the data?

6. According to this chapter, what is the center around which the thesis itself is based?

7. How many of the research questions on the research instrument should be given some type of statistical treatment?

8. What does the instrumentation section of Chapter Three of the thesis identify?

9. For the student who has not written a thesis, what section of the methodology is frequently the most difficult to write?

10. According to this chapter, what is the first step in the interpretation of the data?

Role Play Exercises

Two students may participate in these role play exercises either outside of class or as in-class exercises. One plays the role of the first student and the other plays the role of the second student. Read the scripts and then pick up the conversations in your own words.

1. FIRST STUDENT: This is probably the hardest part of the thesis for me. What do I actually write in the section on interpreting the data?

   SECOND STUDENT: You are the only person who can make that decision. However, Leedy provides eight guidelines and if you follow these, you will probably find the task far easier.

   FIRST STUDENT: What are they and how did you apply them to your thesis?

   SECOND STUDENT: Let's take them one by one and with each one I will give you an explanation as to how I worked with the guidelines. The first one is to...

   ### Continue on Your Own

2. FIRST STUDENT: I don't understand this narrow and broad sense of interpretation nonsense. Tell me, just what is this research structure section all about? What does it include and how does it relate to the third chapter of my thesis?

   SECOND STUDENT: At first glance it can all be confusing. Let's take your questions one at a time and I think I can help to clarify for you. Starting with your first question, the research structure section...

   ### Continue on Your Own

3. FIRST STUDENT: I understand I need to have some kind of visual with most, if not all of the statistical analyses. However, I really don't understand the difference in visuals and how I go about selecting which visual is most appropriate for each statistical analysis. I know it will take you far too much time to counsel me on the appropriate visual for each statistical analysis. Where can I turn to get some help?

SECOND STUDENT: There are several resources and I suggest that you turn to them right away. Probably the best resource is...

Continue on Your Own

9.1. Research Methodologies Draft

Review the information in this chapter concerning the writing of the research methodologies section of Chapter Three. Based on this review, prepare a draft of the research methodologies for your thesis. Be sure to include one or more paragraphs on each of the following: the research population, the research design, the treatment of the data, instrumentation, and data analysis. Type your name at the top of the research methodologies draft.

To your completed research methodologies draft, attach an Instructor Comment Sheet. Make sure the Instructor Comment Sheet has the Assignment section filled in and that it has your name on it. Place the research methodologies draft and the Instructor Comment Sheet into an 8.5" × 11" manila envelope with a clasp flap with your name typed on the envelope. If your instructor requests it, include a blank, top-quality audiotape (30 minutes long) with your name printed on it, so that your professor may give you feedback.

9.2. Draft of Means of Obtaining Data and Location of Data

Review the information in this chapter and from your research concerning the writing of the means of obtaining data and the location of data sections of Chapter Three. Based on this review, prepare a draft of the means of obtaining data and the location of data sections of your thesis. Be sure to address the means of obtaining data as it relates to each problem and subproblem; be sure to address the location of data as it relates to each problem and subproblem. Type your name at the top of each page of these drafts.

To your completed means of obtaining data draft and your completed location of data draft, attach an Instructor Comment Sheet. Make sure the Instructor Comment Sheet has the Assignment section filled in and that it has your name on it. Place the two drafts and the Instructor Comment Sheet into an 8.5" × 11" manila envelope with a clasp flap with your name typed on the envelope. If your instructor requests it, include a blank, top-quality audiotape (30 minutes long) with your name printed on it, so that your professor may give you feedback.

9.3. Draft List of Item Analysis Statistical Treatments and Accompanying Visuals

Type your name at the top of the next page. In the spaces provided, type (double-spaced) the information called for. Note that this information will be needed for each item (question) on the research instrument. The sheet on the next page provides only enough lines for the first few research questions; more sheets will probably be needed. In continuing the exercise to its conclusion (until all questions on the research instrument have been addressed), use additional pages. Photocopy as many blank copies of the next page as you need, or simply prepare additional pages with the same column headings. Continue listing question numbers, the statistical treatment for each, and the visual(s) for each, until one or more lines have been completed for all questions on your research instrument. Type your name on each sheet, and staple all sheets together before handing them in.

Before preparing this assignment, review this chapter, your own research, and one or more textbooks on statistics. To the draft list of item analysis statistical treatments and accompanying visuals, attach an Instructor Comment Sheet. Make sure the Instructor Comment Sheet has the Assignment section filled in and that it has your name on it. Place the completed list and the Instructor Comment Sheet into an 8.5" × 11" manila envelope with a clasp flap with your name typed on the front of the envelope. If your instructor requests it, include a blank, top-quality audiotape (30 minutes long) with your name on it, so that your professor may give you feedback.

Draft List of Item Analysis Statistical Treatments and Accompanying Visuals

On the lines below, identify the statistical treatment to be applied to the research instrument item (question) numbered. Next to the identified treatment, indicate the type of visual(s) you plan to use in conjunction with that statistical treatment for the research instrument item question being considered. Follow this process for all questions on your research instrument (your questionnaire). You will need to use additional pages in order to continue listing question numbers, statistical treatments, and visuals. Follow the process in the same order as it is followed on this sheet, starting with research question number 10 and continuing as needed. Type your name on each sheet and staple all sheets together before handing them in.

Q # Statistical Treatment   Visual(s)

1. _____   _____

2. _____   _____

3. _____   _____

4. _____   _____

5. _____   _____

6. _____   _____

7. _____   _____

8. _____   _____

9. _____   _____

Chapter Three— The Mechanics

$\mathbf{U}$*pon completion of this chapter, you will be able to:*

1. Complete the preparation of thesis mailing materials.

2. Write a first draft of Chapter Three of your thesis.

3. Update Chapter Two of your thesis by preparing a second draft.

4. Compare the advantages and disadvantages of coding research instruments and/or the return envelopes in which completed questionnaires are returned to you.

Introduction

Although the bulk of the work on Chapter Three has been finished at this stage, there are several tasks that remain to be completed. These include preparing a title page and an introduction. At the end of Chapter Three a summary section needs to be written. This summary should tie together the first three chapters.

In addition to completing work on Chapter Three, you must prepare the research instrument, envelopes for the instrument, cover letters, and return envelopes. The research instrument is mailed to potential respondents after completing Chapter Three and prior to work on Chapter Four. If research instruments are to be coded, this must be done prior to sending the research instrument to potential respondents. Several factors need to be considered before the research instrument actually goes into the mail; the instrument, the cover letter, and the envelopes all need to be prepared in accordance with established guidelines.

The Chapter Three Title Page and Introduction

The Chapter Three title page is prepared in a manner similar to that in which the title pages of Chapters One and Two were prepared. Centered approximately a third of the way down the page in capital letters are the words CHAPTER THREE. Skip four lines and center the title: "Data and the Treatment of the Data," "The Research Design," or "Research Methods," depending on the preferences of your department or educational institution. Check with your professor to determine which title is preferred. These two lines and the appropriate page number are all that appear on the title page of Chapter Three.

The introduction to Chapter Three should be titled "Introduction," and it should start with a review of the research question, the hypotheses, the problems, and the subproblems. It should have a transition paragraph stating that whereas the literature review in Chapter Two has identified appropriate secondary source data designed to address the research question, its hypotheses, and its problems, primary data will also be drawn upon, and Chapter Three will identify what primary data is being sought and how you plan to obtain that data. In other words, this paragraph is a transition between Chapter Two and the body of Chapter Three.

Preparing the Mailing and Mail Considerations for the Research Instrument

You will need to prepare several pieces for the mailing. These include (1) the printed research instrument; (2) a cover letter (which will be enclosed with the research instrument); (3) a self-addressed, stamped return envelope; (4) mailing labels containing the addresses of the potential respondents; and (5) envelopes for mailing the research instrument, cover letter, and return envelope to each potential respondent.

As stressed in Chapter 7 (when the research instrument was introduced), the printed research instrument should be prepared in such a way that it will encourage the respondent to complete and return the questionnaire. The best design from the standpoint of getting responses is to have a short questionnaire that includes few questions (often no more than 10) and appears on one side of one page. When confronted with such a short questionnaire, and especially when it is accompanied by a self-addressed, stamped envelope, a potential respondent will be more likely to complete and return the questionnaire than a person who receives a 30-page questionnaire with no self-addressed, stamped envelope.

Most questionnaires, however, will be substantially longer than 10 questions, and no matter how you structure the questions on the page, you will find that it is not possible to get the entire questionnaire on a single sheet of paper. One solution is to use a single large sheet of paper, folded over and printed on both sides. Standard letterhead is 8.5" × 11" in size. If you use a 17" × 11" sheet, it can be folded in half and printed on both sides. This provides the illusion of a one- or two-page questionnaire, but it gives you four pages to use in listing research questions. Most researchers can easily fit between 40 and 50 research questions onto a questionnaire of this size when the questions are typeset and the printer slightly reduces the size of the print.

An additional advantage to using a 17" × 11" sheet of paper folded in half is that if there are fewer than 30 questions, you may be able to use the front sheet as the cover letter, preprinting the letter and leaving room for the name and address to be typed in after the page is printed. When this is done, instead of having a research instrument and a cover letter included in each mailing, you will have only one sheet of paper. Dillman, however, points out that printing the cover letter on the questionnaire may lower response rates (Dillman, 1978, p. 262). Whatever approach you use, the questionnaire should be typeset and kept to as few pages as possible.

As pointed out in Chapter 7, the cover letter needs to be brief and to the point. It should never exceed one page in length. The purpose of the cover letter is to introduce the research instrument to the reader and to ask the potential respondent to complete and return the research instrument. It is important, especially when sensitive information is requested, to identify your academic affiliation and to make the potential respondent comfortable in releasing data that may be considered confidential.

The cover letter, therefore, should start by identifying your college or university and stating that the completion of the attached questionnaire would be appreciated. Here is an example: "Each year the hospitality program (insert the name of your program) at (insert the name of your college or university) encourages students to undertake original research that will be of benefit to the industry as a whole or to those working in specific segments of the industry. The attached research questionnaire is designed to elicit data to address the following research question: (insert your research question). It would be appreciated if you would complete the questionnaire by neatly printing or typing responses to each question. Upon completion, please return the completed questionnaire in the self-addressed, stamped envelope provided."

Several points of potential concern to the respondent should be addressed in the cover letter. For example, if you think the data may be considered confidential or the potential respondent might not want to release data associated with the name of his or her company, a paragraph in the cover letter should address confidentiality by stating something like this: "It is recognized that the confidentiality of data or the affiliation of data to specific companies may be an issue. Therefore, the questionnaire and the attached envelope have not been coded in any manner. Please rest assured that there will be no way of tracking individual responses or matching them to specific individuals or firms. In addition, the data will be summarized for all respondents, and no single response or set of data will be identified or highlighted in any way." A statement along these lines should resolve any concern for confidentiality.

Some respondents will want to have a copy of the data that have been developed. Offer to provide a copy of the synopsis of the study when it is completed, if the respondent wishes to receive it. The technique for providing this should keep in mind the fact that some of the respondents may also be concerned about the confidentiality of data.

There are two ways of handling this issue. One is to send a copy of the synopsis to everyone who receives the questionnaire. State that whether or not the respondent completes and returns the questionnaire, a copy of the synopsis will be provided. This suggests that no record will be kept of those who send back completed questionnaires, which should reassure anyone who is concerned about the confidentiality of data.

Another approach is to request that the respondent include his or her business card with the response if a copy of the synopsis is requested. State that business cards will then be filed separately and be completely removed from questionnaire responses. Inform the potential respondent that when the synopsis has been completed, copies will be mailed to all who sent their business cards.

The second approach is less expensive in terms of reproduction and mailing costs than the first and is easy to accomplish. However, it may concern some potential respondents, who might believe that their business card will be kept with the completed questionnaire (and thereby compromise confidentiality). Your cover letter should stress that this will not happen, but there may still be some who are concerned, and who would then either not respond at all or provide incorrect data in their responses. It is a less expensive alternative, but it is a slightly more risky alternative.

Thank the respondent in advance for completing the questionnaire, and indicate a deadline by which the questionnaire should be completed and returned. These two points can be addressed in a single sentence. For example: "The analysis of the data will commence on (insert the deadline for sending back completed questionnaires) and your assistance in providing completed questionnaire responses by that date is very much appreciated." This is usually the last sentence in the letter. Close with "Sincerely" or "Very truly yours" and be sure to show "Encl. Research Questionnaire" at the bottom of the letter.

I advise you to include a self-addressed, stamped envelope, so that the potential respondent will have an easy and cost-free method of returning the completed questionnaire. The size of the envelope is important. The questionnaire and cover letter are usually on 8.5" × 11" paper, which is folded to fit into a standard-size envelope. The standard envelope is eight and three-fourths inches long. The return envelope, therefore, needs to be approximately one-eighth of an inch shorter in length and is usually one-sixteenth of an inch shorter in width than the standard-size envelope. It is sufficiently large to hold the research instrument, but is small enough to fit into the standard-size envelope. When purchasing the return envelopes, tell the sales clerk how you plan to use the envelopes, so that you will be certain to get envelopes of the correct size. Open the box of envelopes before you leave the store and place a return envelope into a standard-size envelope to make certain that the return envelopes are the correct size. It is also important that the research instrument be folded on an automatic folder. Inform the printer that the fold needs to be tight; if it is off by much, the research instrument will be too wide to fit into the return envelope.

An easier option is to use a regular-size business envelope as the return envelope. Folded, it will fit into the envelope mailed to potential respondents. This, however, presents a less professional image to the recipient. Another option is to use a legal-size envelope for the outside envelope and a regular-size envelope for the return envelope. Consider the alternatives and choose the one that fits you best. Of the three, the first option presents the most professional image.

If your research instrument is lengthy, or if anything other than the research instrument, cover letter, and return envelope need to be placed into the envelope, a standard-size envelope may be too small, and you may need to purchase a slightly larger envelope. Paper supply houses stock envelopes in a wide range of sizes, and some office supply stores stock envelopes in several sizes as well. Put together a sample of each item going into the envelope, and stuff a standard-size envelope with these items to see if a larger one will be needed. If at all possible, though, you should use standard size envelopes; they cost less and are easier to find.

The return envelope and the envelope in which all items are mailed need to have the return address printed on them. If the return address is that of the college or university, the address alone will lend a greater degree of credibility to the study; this will encourage potential respondents to complete and return the questionnaire.

Because it is much less expensive on a per-envelope basis to have a large number of envelopes printed than to have a small batch printed, some academic departments preprint a large number of envelopes and make them available to students at cost. Ask your professor whether or not your academic department makes preprinted envelopes available to students.

When preparing the mailing, it helps to have mailing labels with the names and addresses of potential respondents typed or printed on them; the labels can be affixed directly to the envelopes.

Although there will be less response from mailings sent with preaddressed labels than with hand-addressed envelopes, for large mailings, labels present the only practical way of addressing envelopes. The alternative can be far too time-consuming.

When you request the mailing list, you will be offered the choice of receiving the mailing list on a computer printout or on mailing labels. Mailing labels are more convenient. If the names are received on a computer printout, they need to be retyped onto mailing labels or directly onto the envelopes. Mailing labels come in two varieties: with a backing that must be wet, like a stamp, or with a backing that sticks directly to the envelope. The latter are slightly more expensive, but they provide a much more rapid way of affixing labels. If the mailing list is not available on labels, many student researchers purchase blank labels, type the names and addresses onto the labels, and affix the labels directly to the envelopes. This can be easier and faster than typing the names and addresses onto the envelopes.

Coding Options

Some student researchers will wish to code their research instruments, their return envelopes, or both. Research instruments are coded in order to identify the respondent so that follow-up mailings can be sent to those who do not respond. Instead of asking respondents to enter their names and addresses on the questionnaire, the code identifies them. Coding removes any potential bias in recording data based on who the respondent was, and it eliminates the possibility of respondents leaving out their names or addresses. Of course, if you request sensitive data, and in your cover letter you indicate that the instrument and envelopes are not coded, they should not be. It is unethical to code the research instrument or the envelopes if you say that they are not going to be coded.

The easiest and most frequently used coding is a numerical system, with numbers assigned to each potential respondent in the order in which the potential respondent's name appears on the mailing list. This can be a numeric or alphanumeric coding, entered in ink, handwritten or typed in the top right-hand corner of the questionnaire. (For convenience, you can use a stamp; stamps that affix sequential numbers can be purchased at office supply houses.) The code, of course, can be placed anywhere on the research instrument. However, it is considered more ethical not to try to hide the code, but to show it clearly on the research instrument.

Return envelopes can also be coded. These codes often serve the same purpose. If a numeric or alphanumeric code is used on the return envelope, you can identify respondents before opening the envelopes simply by matching numbers with names. The problem with this is that occasionally, a respondent will send the research instrument back in an envelope other than the return envelope that was provided. This happens rarely, however, and the option of placing the respondent code on the outside of the envelope is being used by an increasing number of student researchers.

Another coding option that is frequently used on return envelopes is a code to identify the student researcher. In many academic departments, all students write theses, and the academic department will frequently be the address for research instrument returns. As noted earlier, such an address lends a greater degree of credibility to the project. The problem from the standpoint of both the student and the department, however, is matching each return envelope with the appropriate student. A coding option used on the return envelope can assist in this process. The coding options most frequently used for this purpose are the initials of the student or a sequential numerical code. The numerical coding system tends to work better. A different, but sequential numerical code (usually three or four digits) is assigned by the department to each student who is writing a thesis. The student searches through the returned envelopes (which are placed in a "student returns" bin) for his or her numerical code. If two students happen to have the same initials, the initialing system can be a problem; with the numerical coding system, no two students will ever have the same code. The student and the department will be able to rapidly match returned envelopes with student researchers.

The student code should appear immediately above, below, or to the right-hand side of the return address. It can be written (in ink), typed, or stamped.

Putting Chapter Three Together

Once the mailing has been prepared, it is time to put Chapter Three together. Chapter Three is probably the most difficult of the chapters to assemble in an organized and complete format. In preparing to put together Chapter Three, it is important to recognize that all aspects of the research methodologies and research structure need to be addressed. The reader needs to come away from Chapter Three with a clear understanding of exactly what you will do in developing original data and how that original data will be tied to secondary data in order to determine the outcomes sought as identified by the subproblems, the problems, the hypotheses, and the research question. Because research methodologies vary, what is appropriate and necessary in one thesis may not be needed in another. Look at all potential ingredients of Chapter Three and include each aspect that will be needed to provide the reader with a clear and complete understanding of what will be done.

A smorgasbord of ingredients may be included in Chapter Three; few theses will include all of them. Sections should be presented in the following order: title page; introduction; the data; primary data; secondary data; coding; population; reliability; validity; research methodologies; data needed; means of obtaining the data for each problem and subproblem (sometimes called "Data Collection"); follow-up; location of the data for each problem and subproblem; screening of the data for each problem and subproblem; criteria for the admissibility of data for each problem and subproblem; treatment of the data for each problem and subproblem; interpretation of the data for each problem and subproblem; item analyses for each research question; statistical treatments for each research item analyzed, each subproblem, each problem, and each hypothesis; tables, figures, graphs, and/or charts for each research item analyzed, each problem and/or subproblem analyzed, and each hypothesis considered; chapter summary; and chapter bibliography.

Creating a Three-Chapter Package

Once Chapters One, Two, and Three and the research instrument mailing have been completed, you have crossed a threshold: from the preparation for the thesis to the analysis of the data and the writing of the thesis. Everything that has been done up to this point has been preparatory in nature.

It is, therefore, appropriate at the end of Chapter Three to tie together the three chapters in an overall summary that identifies, in one or two paragraphs, the major points brought out in each of the three chapters and in the research instrument mailing. The best way to prepare this three-chapter summary is to review the chapter summaries and condense these into a one- or two-paragraph overall summary. Add highlights of the planned research instrument mailing.

Once the three-chapter summary has been completed and the research instrument mailing has been sent out, the preparatory work is finished. You can now turn your attention to incoming responses from the research instrument mailing, the analysis of the data, and the interpretation of the data—the tasks that form the nucleus of Chapters Four and Five.

Summary

The focus of this chapter is on the mechanics of Chapter Three, starting with the title page and introduction. The title page contains the chapter number, the title ("Data and the Treatment of the Data," "The Research Design," or, "Research Methods") and the page number. The introduction to Chapter Three should be a transition between Chapter Two and the body of Chapter Three.

The next part of this chapter deals with preparing the mailing, the research instrument, and the cover letter. The research instrument and the cover letter were introduced in Chapter 7 and are discussed in greater detail in this chapter. Exercises in Chapter 7 called for the preparation of a draft research instrument and a draft cover letter. By reviewing the material in this chapter, you can add to and finalize the research instrument and cover letter drafts so that they will be ready to mail out.

The mailing consists of five pieces: the research instrument, the cover letter, the return envelope, the address labels (one for the return envelope and one for the envelope sent to the potential respondent), and the envelope in which the entire mailing is sent.

The research instrument should be one or at most a very few pages. It can be printed on an oversize sheet of paper if necessary, folded to provide four letter-size sides. All four sides can be used for research questions, or one can be used for the cover letter and the other three for research questions.

The cover letter should be no more than one page long and should establish your academic affiliation. It should point out the expected benefit of the study. Points of concern, such as the confidentiality of data and the availability of study outcomes through a synopsis, should be addressed. Thank the potential respondent in advance and ask that the completed questionnaire be returned by a stated deadline. Include a self-addressed, stamped envelope for the return of the questionnaire.

Check with your academic department to determine whether or not envelopes are made available through the department; these are usually less expensive when academic departments buy them in bulk. Several types of coding options are presented in this chapter, but do not code if you have stated that coding will not be used.

The final portion of this chapter relates to the assembly of Chapter Three. It identifies the order in which sections of Chapter Three are to be placed. Although not all chapters will have exactly the same ingredients, the order of placement of the sections should be as presented in this chapter.

Before concluding the chapter, a summary to the first three chapters of the thesis should be written. This may be a separate section or it may be a paragraph following the standard end-of-chapter summary. Because the first three chapters represent the conclusion of all preparatory work, it is appropriate to include a section tying together Chapters One, Two, and Three.

Bibliography

Dillman, Don A. *Mail and Telephone Surveys: The Total Design Method.* New York: John Wiley & Sons, 1978.

Discussion Questions

These questions may be discussed by two or more students outside of class, or they may be discussed during class for a more wide-ranging discussion.

1. In addition to the page number, what appears on the other two lines that constitute the title page of Chapter Three?

2. According to this chapter, when is the preparatory work on the thesis finished?

3. The introduction to Chapter Three can be considered to be a transition. It is a transition between what two bodies of written material in the thesis?

4. Which chapter of the thesis is probably the most difficult of the chapters to put together in an organized and complete format?

5. There are several components in the mailing to potential respondents. What are these components?

6. If return envelopes are coded, where should the code be placed?

7. According to this chapter, what is the best design for the questionnaire?

8. What is the easiest and most frequently used coding system for matching completed questionnaires received from respondents with the name of the respondent?

9. According to this chapter, with what information should the cover letter start?

10. Why do many students prefer to purchase blank labels and then type the names and addresses from the mailing list onto the labels, rather than type the names and addresses directly onto the envelopes?

Role Play Exercises

Two students may participate in these role play exercises either outside of class or as in-class exercises. One plays the role of the first student and the other plays the role of the second student. Read the scripts and then pick up the conversations in your own words.

1. FIRST STUDENT: I'm not sure I understand how printing this research instrument works when I am going to use a large sheet of folded paper. It seems more cumbersome than just having the printer photocopy several pages. What is the difference?

   SECOND STUDENT: The first is a major difference in impression on the recipient between something that is typed and photocopied and a questionnaire that is typeset and printed. However, to address your question regarding the use of a 17" × 11" sheet that is folded...

   ### Continue on Your Own

2. FIRST STUDENT: I thought I understood how to put together Chapter Three and then I read that not all of the ingredients had to be included, but when they are included, they have to be in a specific order. I just don't understand. What needs to be included and what doesn't? In what order do I need to prepare the components of Chapter Three?

   SECOND STUDENT: Based on my research, it seems that tradition dictates a specific order. However, because each thesis is different from every other thesis, a few sections of Chapter Three may not be appropriate for a few theses. Let's start by identifying the order in which sections should be sequenced, and then I'll point out a few of the sections that may not be absolutely essential for every thesis. The sequencing starts with...

   ### Continue on Your Own

3. FIRST STUDENT: This thing about codes smacks of cloak and dagger connotations. I really don't like the idea of hiding codes all over the envelopes and questionnaire. Why should I be so sneaky?

   SECOND STUDENT: The concept of utilizing codes is an established concept in both academic and industry research. Codes can serve a very real purpose. Let me explain the options and how they work and I think you will agree. Probably the most frequently used code is utilized in order to . . .

Continue on Your Own

10.1. Completed Ready-to-Mail Mailing

Prepare the mailing of your questionnaires, cover letters, and return envelopes stuffed in envelopes addressed to all persons on your mailing list. Do not seal the envelopes. Place them in envelope boxes or boxes of a similar size. Set up an appointment with your professor, so that your mailing can be checked before the envelopes are sealed and you deliver the mailing to the post office.

Before meeting with your professor, review the information in this chapter and in the other chapters which relate to the preparation of mailings. Prepare an Instructor Comment Sheet and bring it with you to the meeting with your professor. Make sure the Instructor Comment Sheet has the Assignment section filled in and that it has your name on it. When you give your professor your mailing to check, give him the Instructor Comment Sheet in an 8.5" × 11" manila envelope with a clasp flap with your name typed on the front of the envelope. (You do not need to include an audiotape; your professor will be able to tell you about any problems in person.)

10.2. Chapter Three

Review Chapters 7 through 10. Based on the information in these chapters and your own research, prepare Chapter Three of your thesis. Type your name at the top of each page.

Unless you provide justification for not including one or more of them, the following sections should be included: (1) Chapter Three title page, (2) introduction, (3) the data, (4) primary data, (5) secondary data, (6) coding, (7) population, (8) reliability, (9) validity, (10) research methodologies, (11) data needed and means of obtaining the data for each problem and subproblem, (12) follow-up, (13) location of the data for each problem and subproblem, (14) screening of the data for each problem and subproblem, (15) criteria for the admissibility of data for each problem and subproblem, (16) treatment of the data for each problem and subproblem, (17) interpretation of the data for each problem and subproblem, (18) item analyses for each research question, (19) statistical treatments for each research item analyzed, each subproblem, each problem, and each hypothesis, (20) tables, figures, graphs, and/or charts for each research item analyzed, each problem and/or subproblem analyzed, and each hypothesis considered, (21) chapter summary, and (22) chapter bibliography. Make certain that there are smooth transitions between sections throughout the chapter. Type your name at the top of each page of Chapter Three.

To your completed chapter, attach an Instructor Comment Sheet. Make sure the Instructor Comment Sheet has the Assignment section filled in and that it has your name on it. Place Chapter Three and the Instructor Comment Sheet into an 8.5"× 11" manila envelope with a clasp flap with your name typed on the envelope. If your instructor requests it, include a blank, top-quality audiotape (30 minutes long) with your name printed on it, so that your professor may give you feedback.

10.3. Chapter Two Update

Review your second draft of Chapter Two and all sections in Chapters 7 through 10 that relate to Chapter Two. Conduct a review of literature that has been published since you last addressed Chapter Two. Finally, review your instructor's comments regarding your first and second drafts of Chapter Two of your thesis. Based on these, prepare an update of Chapter Two. Type your name at the top of each page.

To your completed Chapter Two update, attach an Instructor Comment Sheet. Make sure the Instructor Comment Sheet has the Assignment section filled in and that it has your name on it. Place the update of Chapter Two and the Instructor Comment Sheet into an 8.5" × 11" manila envelope with a clasp flap with your name typed on the envelope. If your instructor requests it, include a blank, top-quality audiotape (30 minutes long) with your name printed on it, so that your professor may give you feedback.

CHAPTER ELEVEN

Mailings and Chapter Four

U*pon completion of this chapter, you will be able to:*

1. Schedule research instrument mailings, mailing follow-ups, and the writing of Chapters Four and Five and the appendix.

2. Report the outcomes of research instrument mailings.

3. Discuss the philosophical differences relating to questionnaire response attachments being considered original data.

4. Write Chapter Four of your thesis.

Introduction

After Chapter Three has been completed, it is time to mail the questionnaires. The timing and distribution of the mailing is discussed in this chapter.

After receiving responses from the mailing, the responses are tabulated and statistical analyses are conducted based on response data. It is then time to write Chapter Four. Most of this chapter relates to the process of preparing for and writing Chapter Four.

Time Constraints

Students who are enrolled in a two-semester program designed to guide them through their thesis are, perhaps, in the best position as it relates to the timing of the mailing of the questionnaire. They can mail on the second or third of January, have their questionnaire received at a time when most hospitality businesses are not as busy as they may be in the period before or during the holidays and at a time when a vacationing recipient will be finished with the holidays and back at work. They also often have the advantage that the break between semesters typically lasts until the middle or end of January, so two or three weeks will be available for the return of questionnaire responses before the new semester begins. If the return address on the questionnaire is that of the college or university, you can return to classes expecting some responses to be waiting.

If you are enrolled in a one-semester program (during which all five chapters will need to be written) you will be faced with much tighter time constraints. It will still take two to three weeks before the bulk of responses are received, and none of that time should fall during the Thanksgiving holidays. Therefore, those enrolled in a one-semester program will need to start working on the development of the questionnaire early in the academic term. Those enrolled in a college or university that operates on a quarter-term basis will be faced with even tighter time constraints and will need to watch their time still more carefully.

In planning the mailing and the thesis completion calendar, work backwards on the timing. It will take a minimum of one or two weeks each to prepare Chapters Four and Five, and your professor will need some time to review these chapters. Give yourself at least three weeks to receive responses to the mailing and a minimum of 10 days for the printing and distribution of the questionnaire and cover letter.

The Mechanics of Questionnaire Mailing

Ask your professor about the questionnaire mailing mechanics that apply to your department or college. Colleges and universities have varying policies regarding mailings. In some cases, the college will prefer that the mailing be from the school, and—especially if it is a state college—the institution will often pick up the cost of the postage. When this is the case, college and university mail rooms usually require that your departmental code be indicated on envelopes, so that your department can be billed. They may require that mail be bundled, usually by zip code, in groups of 10 pieces or more. This usually means rubber banding each batch of 10 pieces or more that is going to the same zip code. Make certain that you understand and follow regulations if you use college or university mailing facilities.

Envelopes should always be typed or have typed or printed labels. Information should include the full name of the recipient, followed by the title of the recipient, the company name, street address, city, state, and zip code (preferably the 13-number zip code). Address labels can be used, but mail that has an address label on it is more subject to being thrown away without being opened than mail with the address directly typed on the envelope. The return address should always be shown; if it is agreeable with your college, use the college return address. The return address should show your name, code number, or initials (usually in the upper left-hand corner above the college address), and it should include your department name and any intra-college postal directions (such as an academic box number).

Bundle the contents by stapling the cover letter to the questionnaire and folding the entire mailing (see Figure 11.1). If you have a multipage questionnaire, the printer can pre-fold it. When this is the case, the cover letter should be folded separately and placed before the questionnaire in the stack of material that is enclosed in the envelope.

The return envelope should be on the bottom of the stack. As pointed out in Chapter 10, it should be small enough to fit in the mailing envelope without having to be folded, yet large enough to hold the return questionnaire without the return questionnaire having to be folded smaller than the standard three-fold.

Return envelopes should be hand-stamped in advance. A real stamp, rather than a postage meter stamp strip, should be used. If a unique stamp is purchased, such as a commemorative, this will draw attention to the stamp and it may add to the potential of the questionnaire being completed and returned.

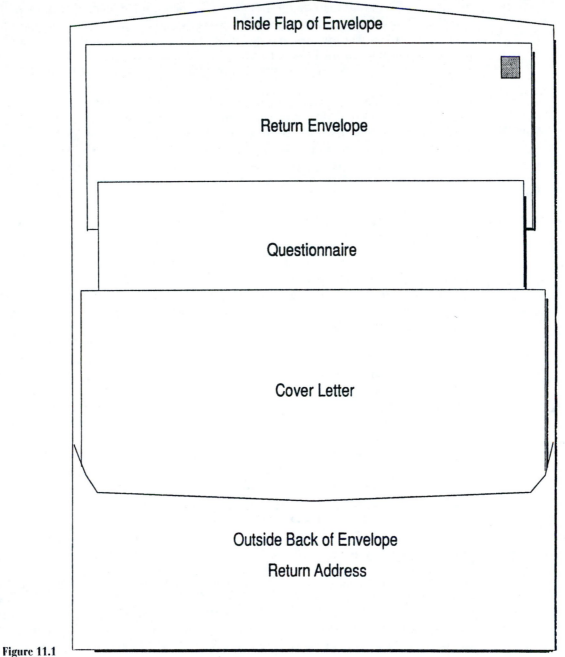

Figure 11.1

Second Mailing

Second (and sometimes third) mailings should be considered and planned in advance. If an insufficient number of responses are received as a result of the first mailing, the second mailing will serve as a reminder to those who have not yet responded. If the study is a blind study (that is, one in which the respondents are unidentified), the follow-up mailing will have to go to all potential respondents. If this is the case, appropriate wording of the cover letter is necessary. Here is an example: "A few weeks ago, a research study mailing was sent to you with a questionnaire that we asked you to complete.

Because it was a blind mailing there is no way to determine whether or not you have responded. If you have already responded, thank you. If not, it would be appreciated if you would take a few minutes and complete the attached questionnaire, returning it in the self-addressed, stamped envelope provided."

If the mailing is coded, you will know which of the people who were mailed the questionnaire have responded and which ones have not. Here is an example of a follow-up letter to a coded mailing: "Our records indicate that we have not yet received a response from you. Your ideas are very important and will contribute substantially to the validity of this study. It would be appreciated if you would take a few minutes and answer the very few questions on the attached questionnaire, returning it in the self-addressed, stamped envelope provided. Of course, if our correspondence has crossed in the mail, please do not respond a second time—and thank you."

When to Start the Data Analysis

Working under time constraints to complete Chapter Four, there is a tendency to want to start the data analysis as soon as the first questionnaire returns are received. In most cases, however, the analysis of the data cannot be completed until a sufficient number of returns have been received. Unfortunately, recipients of questionnaire mailings do not always return them right away. Typically, the majority of returns are received within three weeks of the mailing. If the returns are light and there is an insufficient number from which to generalize results in a statistically significant manner, a second mailing is usually sent out approximately three weeks after the first. However, if a significant response is received within the first three weeks, you should set a cut-off date for receipt of responses and use only those received by that date. It is usually best to advise recipients of the questionnaire that completed questionnaires should be returned by a specific date.

Before starting the data analysis, you can initiate a categorization of questionnaire responses. If this is done on a computer, the response data for each questionnaire item number can be tabulated and computed. Initial analyses can be run as data are entered from one batch of completed questionnaires to the next. You will save a substantial amount of time if you enter data as completed questionnaires are received, rather than waiting until all expected questionnaires are received.

Recording Incoming Data

When data are received (that is, when completed questionnaires are returned), incoming data may be recorded using note cards or using a computer. Note cards take much longer, but the process can be completed with as high a degree of quality as it can with computers. If you use a computer or word processor, the task is much more easily accomplished. Data can be stored and retrieved more rapidly and manipulated much faster.

However the data are recorded, a separate page or card should be devoted to each item on the questionnaire. In most cases, a simple tabulation of responses is sufficient, especially if there is no free-flow information. If free-flow information is requested (several words, phrases, or sentences), it is likely that more than one note card or computer page will be needed. In this case, review the responses to the question on all returned questionnaires, group responses by type or category of response, and record all of a similar category on the note card with the appropriate label, moving to a different note card or computer page with each category heading. A synopsis or overview of the responses may be appropriate for the individual question item; if this is the case, use a separate note card or page for recording the overview. Review computer program options. Some programs, especially those with a built-in thesaurus, can sort free-flow data by key words and can match similar key words.

Applying Statistical Data Analyses

Statistical analyses of the data should be prepared for each research questionnaire item. Usually, only one statistical application will be appropriate for each item. However, more than one statistical application will sometimes be appropriate. When this is the case, you may either choose between the statistical approach options, taking only one option as appropriate, or you may elect to adopt more than one statistical option. Remember that the statistical options adopted should have been identified and discussed in Chapter Three of the thesis. It is considered inappropriate to make a change in, to add, or to delete statistical applications during the processing phase (after completed questionnaires are received) or while writing Chapter Four.

A point of caution is in order. Your statistical analyses may reveal one or more trends that do not agree with your hypothesis. Do not eliminate, change, or ignore these data or trends. Your hypothesis might be wrong. Whether it is right or wrong, data and statistical trends that do not agree with your hypotheses must still be presented in the body of Chapter Four. When writing Chapter Five, they should be reconciled based on research parameters or recognized as separate points of view.

Preparing the Charts

In preparing the charts that accompany the statistical analyses for each of the research question items, several factors should be kept in mind. These include visual clarity, evenness of numerical spacing, and labeling. Visual clarity can be a problem with both hand-drawn charts and computer-prepared charts. The chart must be clear enough that the reader can immediately see the lines and sections on it. Bar or pie charts that have different types of shading reflecting various data categories can be effective if the contrast in design or shading is substantial. However, if you include five, six, or more data categories, some of which have similar design or shading, the reader may easily get confused or misinterpret data. It is better to redesign the chart than to prepare one that can be confusing or misunderstood.

The numbers at the bottom and side of each graph or chart should be spaced consistently throughout each graph in the chapter. They should also be consistent within the graph or chart. For example, you should not skip from a 10-point range to a 50-point or 100-point range. You should have the numbers, 10, 20, 30, 40, 50, 60, 70, 80, 90, and 100 at the bottom with even spaces between one another. The same should apply on the vertical graph. In some cases, data will not easily lend itself to having the same numerical spacings throughout Chapters Four and Five. When this is the case, a variation from the standard that is used in the chapter should be provided, with a note explaining the variation and the reasons for it. This note will usually be in the context of the data rather than directly on the graph or chart, but sometimes it will appear on the chart or graph itself.

Labeling is perhaps the most frequently encountered problem when you consider graphs, charts, figures, and tables. You should understand what it is that is being measured, and you should convey this in not more than four or five words in a title. This title should be clearly identified in capital letters or bold letters at the top. A good test of your ability to do this is to show the completed visual to several people who are totally unfamiliar with the study and ask them what they understand the visual to be portraying. If they are able to explain what you intended for the visual to convey, the label or title is probably a good one and should be kept. If, on the other hand, several people identify something different than you planned to convey, or they misinterpret the visual, the labeling or titles should be reconsidered. Unfortunately, many students who prepare theses do not apply this simple test; the end result is that there is often misunderstanding on the part of the reader.

Writing the Chapter Four Front Pages

After completing the body of Chapter Four, it is time to prepare the preliminary and end-of-chapter pages. There are several preliminary pages or sections prior to the body of the chapter that must be written. These include an introduction to the chapter; a restatement of the research question, the hypotheses, the problems, and the subproblems; and an introduction to how the research question items relate to and interface with the subproblems, the problems, the hypotheses, and the research question.

The introduction to the chapter is the first section that is written. It will explain why the chapter is being written and the process or flow that is to be found in Chapter Four. It will briefly review the introductory sections, and it will explain in some detail how the analyses will build from the research instrument items up to the research question itself. Finally, it will note that a summary or a conclusion will be included and will explain in a few sentences what the summary or conclusion will contain.

The next section of the introductory pages is a brief restatement of the research question, the hypotheses, the problems, and the subproblems. In this section, some researchers also identify the research instrument questions that apply to each of the subproblems, problems, and hypotheses. This listing (and the relationships between each of these) can be referred back to at appropriate times throughout the chapter.

The final part of the introductory pages is a brief overview of how each of the research question items interrelate with the problems, the subproblems, the hypotheses, and the research question. You can do this by simply listing research question items by item number and stating that these item numbers relate to the appropriate subproblem. After the item numbers and subproblems have been identified for each of the subproblems, a similar treatment is given to identifying the range of item numbers and subproblems that relate to each problem. This same approach is taken in identifying the item numbers, subproblems, and problems that relate to each hypothesis. Although it may initially appear that a considerable amount of writing will be needed in order to do this, you need devote no more than one or two sentences each to these listings of item numbers and subproblems, problems, and hypotheses.

Preparing the Appendixes

The appendixes for Chapter Four will vary depending on the preferences of your professor. Some instructors prefer to have all original returned questionnaires constitute an appendix to Chapter Four. Others want these at the end of the thesis as a thesis appendix rather than a chapter appendix. Some academicians consider it inappropriate to include returned questionnaires (either originals or copies) in the bound final thesis at all, especially if questionnaire data are considered confidential. Check with your professor to determine his or her preferences.

A wide range of other appendixes can be included. These may be items that are sent along with the completed questionnaire. In some cases, such items add substantially to Chapter Four. For example, with the completed questionnaires several who responded to a study of hotel front desk policies attached copies of pertinent sections from their policy and procedure manuals. Study any documents received from respondents and any other items that may be considered as appendixes to Chapter Four and make a decision to include them or not based on the degree to which you feel that the items are relevant.

Most academicians consider such materials to be part of the results of the study and will present them in Chapter Four, discuss them in Chapter Five, and include them in an appendix to the thesis itself. Of course, you never know what will be received with returned questionnaires; so value judgments will have to be made. Check with your professor if you are not sure how to handle one or more items received with the returned questionnaires.

Many theses will have no appendixes to Chapter Four; others may have as many as six or seven appendixes. The number of appendixes will vary with the subject area and with the materials that have been gathered.

Writing the Chapter Four Conclusion

The conclusion to Chapter Four should briefly summarize the statistical results. Be careful to avoid editorialism; opinions should not be included anywhere in Chapter Four. This is a place for facts that have been brought out by the statistical analyses. Conclusions can and should be drawn from these facts. However, these are conclusions that can be justified and backed up by the statistical facts rather than by opinion. This is an area where many students make the mistake of reaching conclusions that are opinions rather than statistically based conclusions. I recommend that you trade concluding statements with other students, each one reviewing the conclusions developed by one or more other students so that more than one person analyzes the concluding summary and so that one or more reviews can be received from persons who are not intimately involved in the study itself. This should help eliminate editorialism.

Creating a Four-Chapter Package

Chapters One through Four form a package that is now complete except for Chapter Five, the appendixes, and the preliminary pages. Review each of the chapters to make certain that they are exactly as you wish to have them prior to turning them in. Give special attention to Chapter Two and to reviewing any materials that may have been published since the last time Chapter Two was considered.

A Chapter Two revision at this time may also include any references that may have been brought to light as a result of editorial copy or attachments included with the completed questionnaires. It is often appropriate to include editorial comments from individuals who have written a letter accompanying (or even jotted down appropriate comments on) the research instrument. Some attachments are more appropriate as appendixes, but in many cases there is no more appropriate place in which to include them than Chapter Two; check with your professor. Most of those who oversee thesis writing at the bachelor's and master's degree level agree that updating Chapter Two throughout the development of the thesis and including editorial comments made in cover letters, attachments, or on the research instrument is not a violation of good research practice. To the contrary, such insertions often constitute major contributions to Chapter Two. Other professors argue that material received as a result of student's mailing constitutes original data and therefore should never appear in Chapter Two. Both philosophies have their proponents and their detractors among academicians. Determine the philosophy of the professor who is directing your research and be guided accordingly.

Summary

This chapter has addressed timing and distribution concerns relating to the mailing, processing concerns relating to responses from the mailing, and the writing of Chapter Four. For those enrolled in a two-semester course, the mailing should be completed by the second or third of January. Those involved in one-semester or one-quarter courses will need to consider the timing by working backwards and allocating enough time for each of the post-mailing thesis activities.

The preparation of the mailing, if postage is paid by the college, should follow the rules and regulations established by the college or university. The bundling of materials going into the envelope should follow a specific and uniform order, and return envelopes should always be hand-stamped in advance. Second and third mailings should be scheduled and planned in advance.

Although the actual analysis of data should be delayed until most or all mailing responses have been received, data input on note cards or into computer programs should be initiated as soon as the first responses are received. It is better to work with computer programs whenever possible; review computer program options to select those most appropriate and most beneficial for the data analysis being undertaken. Charts, graphs, and other visuals need to maintain visual clarity, evenness of numerical spacing, and clear labeling.

After writing the body of Chapter Four (the statistical analysis), you should next consider the front pages. These include an introduction to the chapter and restatements of the research question, the hypotheses, the problems, and the subproblems. It also includes an introduction to the relationship between the research question and the other key components. After completing the introductory pages, go back to the body of Chapter Four. The statistical analyses, the visuals that accompany them, and the explanations of the analyses are inserted, forming the foundation for the body of Chapter Four. The insertion flow exactly follows the sequencing described in Chapter Three. This usually starts with an analysis of research question items that relate directly to one or more subproblems, proceeds to all subproblems relating to a specific problem, works through all problems relating to specific hypotheses, works from one hypothesis or hypothesis group to the next hypothesis or hypothesis group until all hypotheses have been developed, and finally, works from the hypotheses to the research question and a logical resolution to the research question.

Chapter Four may or may not have appendixes. Your professor should be consulted regarding the need to have them. Although some instructors will want the originals of all completed questionnaires to constitute the first appendix to Chapter Four, most prefer that this constitute the first appendix to the thesis as a whole rather than to Chapter Four (and some prefer not to have them included as an appendix at all). Some thesis subjects accumulate several appropriate appendixes for Chapter Four; others lend themselves to no appendixes. Again, discuss potential appendixes with your professor.

The conclusion to Chapter Four should be a brief summary of the statistical results. Avoid editorialism. Keep in mind that with the conclusion of Chapter Four, the thesis is complete except for the Chapter Five interpretation of data, the appendixes, and some of the preliminary pages. Therefore, include one or two paragraphs in the summary to create a four-chapter package for the reader.

This is also the time to go back and review other chapters, especially Chapter Two. In updating Chapter Two, you may wish to include information or material received with the completed questionnaires. There is a philosophical difference as to whether or not this constitutes "original" data, however. Check with your professor and be guided accordingly.

Discussion Questions

These questions may be discussed by two or more students outside of class, or they may be discussed during class for a more wide-ranging discussion.

1. What are the best dates on which to mail research instruments and their cover letters if you are enrolled in a two-semester academic program during which the thesis is to be completed?

2. Why do some academicians believe that references to letters and other material received from respondents in conjunction with completed questionnaires should not be included in Chapter Two?

3. In planning the mailing and the thesis completion calendar, in what direction should you work when considering the timing?

4. According to this chapter, what is a good check to use in order to eliminate the possibility of editorializing in the writing of the Chapter Four summary?

5. Why should a stamp rather than a postage meter mailing strip be used in stamping envelopes for your thesis mailing?

6. What is the best way to determine whether or not the originals of the returned questionnaires should constitute an appendix for Chapter Four or an appendix for the entire thesis?

7. Should you initiate the data analysis as soon as the first questionnaire returns are received?

8. What is explained in the first section of the introduction to Chapter Four?

9. What are two methods by which incoming data from completed questionnaires may be retrieved and recorded?

10. What is the maximum number of words that should be in a title for a chart, graph, figure, or table included in Chapter Four of your thesis?

Role Play Exercises

Two students may participate in these role play exercises either outside of class or as in-class exercises. One plays the role of the first student and the other plays the role of the second student. Read the scripts and then pick up the conversations in your own words.

1. FIRST STUDENT: This chapter tells me I should start doing something with the data as soon as my responses start coming in, but that I shouldn't analyze the data. If I'm not going to analyze it, what should I do with it?

   SECOND STUDENT: The input of data and the analysis of the data are two separate processes. You can start the input of data into a computer program as soon as you receive the first response back. In fact, it is better to do it that way so that you are not pushed with having to input all of the data in just a day or two. However, the data analysis depends on having essentially all of the data available.

   FIRST STUDENT: Well, I can see that it would make it easier if I input data over a period of time, but I don't understand why I can't do an analysis of the data relating to question one one day and an analysis of the data for question two the next day and so forth until everything is finished. This way I can spread it out in the same way as I spread out doing the data input. I realize I will have more questionnaires in at one time than another, but so what?

SECOND STUDENT: That process might make it easier for you, but it would result in the number of questionnaires forming the data base on which you reach conclusions being different for each item on the research instrument. That would create several problems, the most important one of which is...

Continue on Your Own

2. FIRST STUDENT: I'm hoping that a lot of supplementary material will be received with the questionnaire responses. I want to really beef up Chapter Two of my thesis. However, this chapter suggests that anything received might be considered original data and therefore might not be accepted for inclusion in Chapter Two. If I consider supplementary material received with the questionnaire responses as acceptable data for referring to or including in Chapter Two, why isn't my judgment acceptable enough to go ahead and include it?

SECOND STUDENT: There are opposing theories in academia relating to this. Let me explain these and then I'll clarify why you will need to get a ruling from the professor who directs your thesis research. Let's start with...

Continue on Your Own

3. FIRST STUDENT: I've gotten all of the questionnaire responses I expect to get and I'm ready to start writing Chapter Four. I sat down with everything this morning and suddenly realized I don't know where to start or what order to put things in. Help!

SECOND STUDENT: It can seem overwhelming. Let's start first with how to initiate the writing of Chapter Four and then I'll go through with you what goes where in the chapter. Most people start writing Chapter Four by...

Continue on Your Own

11.1. Report on Outcomes of Mailing

Type your name at the top of the next page. In the spaces provided, report the outcomes of your thesis mailing (the questionnaires you sent out) by filling in the appropriate data.

Before preparing this assignment to hand in, review the responses received from your thesis mailing. To the report on outcomes of your thesis mailing, attach an Instructor Comment Sheet. Make sure the Instructor Comment Sheet has the Assignment section filled in and that it has your name on it. Place the completed mailing outcomes report form and the Instructor Comment Sheet into an 8.5" × 11" manila envelope with a clasp flap with your name typed on the front of the envelope. If your instructor requests it, include a blank, top-quality audiotape (30 minutes long) with your name on it, so that your professor may give you feedback.

Mailing Outcomes Report Form

Fill in the lines below by responding with the information requested. Fill in all blank lines, or indicate a reason why the information requested is not available.

1. Date of this report: _____

2. Number of persons to whom a mailing was sent: _____

3. Number of totally completed questionnaires that have been received to date:

   _____

4. Number of partially completed questionnaires that have been received to date:

   _____

5. Title of thesis research question: _____

   _____

6. Identify any problems or points about which you have concerns as related to the response to your thesis mailing.

   _____

   _____

   _____

11.2. Chapter Four

Review this chapter. Based on the information in this chapter and your own research, prepare Chapter Four of your thesis. Be sure to type your name at the top of each page.

Unless you provide justification for not including one of them, the following sections should be included: (1) introduction to the chapter; (2) research question restatement; (3) list of hypotheses, problems, and subproblems; and (4) introduction to the findings (an overview of how the research question items relate to and interface with the subproblems, the problems, the hypotheses, and the research question).

The body of Chapter Four should follow the sequencing described in Chapter Three. Start with an analysis of research question items relating directly to one or more subproblems. Proceed to all subproblems relating to a specific problem. Work through all problems relating to specific hypotheses. Work from one hypothesis or hypothesis group to the next hypothesis or hypothesis group until all hypotheses have been developed. Finally, work from the hypotheses to the research question. Develop and identify a logical resolution to the research question.

Follow the summary to Chapter Four with a brief four-chapter summary. Check with your professor to determine which appendixes to Chapter Four are needed, and include these. Make certain that there is a smooth transition from one section to the next throughout the chapter. Be sure to type your name at the top of each page of Chapter Four.

To your completed chapter, attach an Instructor Comment Sheet. Make sure the Instructor Comment Sheet has the Assignment section filled in and that it has your name on it. Place Chapter Four and the Instructor Comment Sheet into an 8.5" × 11" manila envelope with a clasp flap with your name typed on the envelope. If your instructor requests it, include a blank, top-quality audiotape (30 minutes long) with your name printed on it, so that your professor may give you feedback.

CHAPTER TWELVE

Writing Chapter Five

U*pon completion of this chapter, you will be able to:*

1. Develop interpretations based on the statistical data developed in Chapter Four.

2. Relate the "Importance of the Study" section from Chapter One to the "Contributions of the Study" section in Chapter Five.

3. List study information dissemination techniques appropriate to your thesis.

4. Write Chapter Five of your thesis.

Introduction

Chapter Five is the chapter that most student researchers enjoy writing the most. It includes your interpretation of the results of the research, the conclusion of the study, the contributions of the study, and one or more recommendations for future studies. In this chapter, you may editorialize, but you should base editorial interpretations and comments on the statistical data that was developed in Chapter Four. All editorialism should be directly relevant to your thesis study.

As with other chapters, Chapter Five starts with an introduction. This is usually followed by a summary of global interpretations (that is, interpretations that relate to the study outcomes). After this, each subproblem is discussed, starting with a review of the pertinent research instrument items.

In the same way that Chapter Four flows from the research instrument items to the subproblems to the problems to the hypotheses and then to the research question, the interpretation of the data follows the same flow. The pertinent research items are reviewed, and then conclusions are drawn (backed by research item statistical results). Subproblem result interpretations are based on the individual results of the multiple research instrument items. Once this has been accomplished, you move to an interpretation of the conclusions of each of the hypotheses. This is approached by reviewing the pertinent subproblems and drawing conclusions backed by subproblem results. These conclusions are based on hypotheses result interpretations and on the individual results of appropriate and pertinent subproblems. The conclusions themselves are interpreted based on the problems as they are stated and the research question as it has been posed. The conclusions of all hypotheses are reviewed, and final conclusions, based on these reviews, are discussed for all hypotheses.

The final step in this interpretation of the data is to reach global interpretations of the result of the study itself. This is projecting the study within the parameters of the study and interpreting how the results might affect the industry. Project globally only with caution. A technical application of results beyond the parameters established in the study is contradictory to the basic tenets of well-prepared research. This is usually handled through the provision of a well-written disclaimer followed by placing projections that approach generalizations beyond the parameters of the study only in appropriate sections of Chapter Five.

Closely related to the global interpretations of the study are the recommendations for further study and the contributions of the study. These are the next sections to be addressed. The recommendations for further study are areas relating to your thesis that you have found lacking in previous research. Identify these potential research areas and make specific recommendations for additional research that might be undertaken.

In Chapter One you identified why the study was considered important. In writing the section related to the contributions of the study, go back to the importance section and determine whether or not the study as it has been completed will contribute to the degree that the importance of the study suggests that it will. Since the study was undertaken, additional contributions probably have been identified, and these should be pointed out in this section as well.

The last part of Chapter Five is a conclusion that ties together all five chapters into a five-chapter package. This is a brief but important final section of the thesis.

The Chapter Five Introduction

Chapter Five is started with a brief introduction. This introduction starts with a transition between the end of Chapter Four and the beginning of Chapter Five telling the reader that the results identified in Chapter Four will now be interpreted. The introduction will continue with an overview of the high points or the major interpretations, identifying and stressing a summary of global interpretations. Usually, at least half of the introduction is a listing and a brief discussion of the global interpretations. The global interpretations part of the introduction is usually written after the major sections of Chapter Five, because it is easier to view the global interpretations after having presented the specific interpretations found in Chapter Five. (It is written out of sequence, but it is presented in the introduction, and, therefore, is presented in sequence.) The reader usually finds that by having this overview of global interpretations presented first, it is easier to reference and to understand the specific interpretations in context. By the term "global interpretations," keep in mind that what is meant relates only to the broad interpretations of the outcomes of the study itself, not generalizations from and beyond the study. You may be tempted to generalize beyond the parameters of the study. There are techniques for dealing with such broader generalizations, but the introduction to Chapter Five and the interpretation sections do not constitute the appropriate locations in which to do it.

Interpreting Each Subproblem's Data

In Chapter Four you addressed each subproblem by first identifying the pertinent research items that applied to the subproblem. These research instrument items were statistically analyzed, and usually at least one chart, graph, figure, or table was prepared reflecting the statistical analysis. The statistically based results were then identified. In Chapter Five, you go back to the subproblem research item analysis that was completed in Chapter Four, summarize the statistical result highlights, and interpret these results for the individual research items and for the subproblem. The subproblem interpretations are based on the interpretations of the results of each of the research items. The difference between the treatment of these data in Chapter Four and the treatment of the data in Chapter Five is essentially that in Chapter Four, you identified only statistical and other data-driven results, being careful not to editorialize or to suggest results that were not clearly a statement of the exact data. The result discussions in Chapter Four were direct conclusions based on presentations of numbers, percentages, and other hard data.

In Chapter Five, interpretations of these data are provided. First (in Chapter Four) the percentages, numbers, and other factual results are presented, and then conclusions are drawn. Once the statistical conclusions have been drawn (in Chapter Four), interpretations of the conclusions are presented in Chapter Five. This may originate with a review of the exact facts and move into a review of the fact-based results; in Chapter Five you continue with an interpretation of the results and editorial comment regarding the interpretation (which usually interprets even more broadly).

Because the Chapter Five presentation of conclusions and interpretations is so closely linked with the work that is done in Chapter Four, you can prepare the conclusions and interpretations at the same time that you are preparing the statistical analysis in Chapter Four. These conclusions and interpretations are set aside and not presented in the thesis paper until Chapter Five. Mechanically speaking, then, you can prepare much of Chapter Five at the same time that Chapter Four is being prepared and written. This will save time and energy. You are deeply involved in the statistical analysis of the data and the subproblems while working with Chapter Four, so it is easy to add conclusions and interpretations at that time. If the preparation of this section of Chapter Five is left until after Chapter Four is completed, you will need to go back to Chapter Four—the raw data—and again put yourself into the mindset that will allow you to draw the conclusions and interpretations required for Chapter Five. I recommend the former approach (preparing a draft of this part of Chapter Five while you are preparing Chapter Four); it can save time, energy, and a certain level of frustration.

Interpreting the Conclusion of Each Hypothesis

The process of developing interpretations of conclusions for each hypothesis is similar to that of interpreting the data for each subproblem. Just as it is easier to write the interpretation of subproblem data while you are working on the same section in Chapter Four, it is easier to prepare the interpretation of conclusions for each hypothesis while you are working on the hypotheses conclusions in conjunction with Chapter Four.

The first step is to take each hypothesis and review the pertinent subproblems for that hypothesis. Consider the subproblems, the statistical data developed in conjunction with the subproblem, the results of that data, and the interpretations of that data. Keep in mind that in Chapter Four you identified any material that did not agree with one or more hypotheses. In Chapter Five this material is reconciled based on research parameters (or at least recognized as a separate viewpoint).

The next step is to draw conclusions. These are stated simply as conclusions, often listed in a numerical sequence. Each of these conclusions is supported by a discussion of the subproblem results and the interpretation of those results, showing a logical link between each of the subproblems, the results of each subproblem, and the interpretations of each subproblem as these apply to each and every hypothesis conclusion interpretation.

Interpreting the Conclusions Concerning the Problem and the Research Question

The process followed in interpreting the conclusions regarding the problem and the research question are identical to the processes followed in developing Chapter Five thus far. This is usually not done while Chapter Four is being developed, because this section of Chapter Five draws on the conclusions of hypotheses and, therefore, goes a step beyond the Chapter Four process. Nevertheless, some student researchers are more comfortable in developing this part of Chapter Five while working on the final sections of Chapter Four. The concluding part of Chapter Four is basically a summary; some students feel that developing the problem and research conclusions and interpreting those conclusions while the summary to Chapter Four is being worked on is easier. As noted, however, most prefer to leave this process until the Chapter Five interpretation of the data for each subproblem and the interpretation of the conclusions for each hypothesis are finished.

The process of developing and writing the interpretation of the conclusions for the problem and the research question starts by reviewing the conclusions of all hypotheses and, from these conclusions, drawing overall conclusions for the research problem itself and simultaneously for the research question. These overall conclusions for the problem and the research question are then extended to global interpretations of the results of the overall research study. The global interpretations are usually listed numerically and then treated one by one (one or more paragraphs for each interpretation). This treatment involves a restatement of the global interpretation and then a development of the reasoning and the logic you used based on the data, the subproblem results, the hypotheses results, and the study conclusions. In other words, you don't simply present a list of global interpretations; you support each global interpretation with the data, the results, and the interpretation of the data from the study. This is editorialism, but it is editorialism supported by facts and data. Again, the term "global interpretation" is interpreted in the same way it was when writing the introduction to Chapter Five. It is limited to the outcomes of the study itself and must avoid generalizations beyond the study.

Generalizations beyond the Parameters of the Study

You may be sorely tempted to generalize the results of your study beyond the parameters of the study. In other words, you might want to say that because the conclusions resulting from your study apply within the narrow confines of the study, they therefore also apply throughout the state, throughout the country, or perhaps throughout the world. You might want to say that they apply to all aspects of the industry that even closely relate to some aspect of your study. However, as noted when discussing the writing of the introduction to Chapter Five, applications must be confined to the sample and the circumstances of the study. Applying results beyond the parameters established in the study is contradictory to the basic tenets of quality research. This desire to generalize results versus the need to stay within the confines of the "tenets of quality research" presents a dilemma for many student researchers. It can be frustrating.

The way this conflict is dealt with by those who are experienced in developing research studies is to write disclaimers and then discuss the generalizations in the sections titled "Recommendations for Further Study" and "Contributions of the Study."

The disclaimer should be written in the section in which you interpret the conclusions concerning the problem and the research question. It is most fitting when applied to a discussion of the conclusions concerning the research question. The disclaimer states that the reader should be careful not to interpret the results beyond the parameters of the study itself. Advise the reader that although the results are applicable to the outcomes of the study as it was conducted, any small change in the parameters might have resulted in different outcomes. Therefore, any generalization beyond the study itself would be unwise. Having done this, you can then suggest "potentially valid" generalizations in the "Recommendations for Further Study" and the "Contributions of the Study" sections.

For example, in writing the "Recommendations for Further Study" section, you might include the following statement in order to suggest that your study results could be generalized to French restaurants throughout the United States. "For this study of French restaurants in Houston, it has been concluded that patrons whose average check totaled 20 dollars or less preferred to order wine by the glass. It is suggested that parallel studies be conducted in major cities throughout the United States. If further research conducted in a substantial number of other cities finds similar conclusions, it may someday be possible to accurately generalize the findings of all such studies by concluding that patrons of French restaurants in the United States whose average check total is 20 dollars or less prefer to order wine by the glass."

If you want to show a possible generalization beyond this study within the industry, you might write the following statement in the "Recommendations for Further Study" section of the thesis. "For this study of French restaurants in Houston, it has been concluded that patrons whose average check totaled 20 dollars or less preferred to order wine by the glass. It is suggested that parallel studies be conducted in other major-country theme restaurants in Houston. If further research conducted in a substantial number of German, Italian, and other theme restaurants in Houston finds similar conclusions, it may someday be possible to accurately generalize the findings of all such studies by concluding that patrons of major-country theme restaurants in Houston whose average check totaled 20 dollars or less prefer to order wine by the glass." You might also extend this recommendation to studies of German, Italian, and other such restaurants in other major U.S. cities, and then extend the concluding geographical generalization to major-country theme restaurants throughout the United States.

In writing the "Contributions of the Study" section of the same thesis, you might suggest even more generalizations from your study. After writing all of the contributions of the study itself, you could extend the contributions section by drawing on the potential contributions of this study combined with the contributions of the parallel studies that were suggested in the "Recommendations for Further Study" section. You might write something similar to the following. "This study, combined with the parallel studies suggested in the 'Recommendations for Further Study,' might result in an ability to ultimately show that patrons of major-country theme restaurants in the United States whose average check totaled 20 dollars or less prefer to order wine by the glass. Understanding this, the proprietors of these restaurants might be able to increase their profits and change their approaches toward selling wine in their restaurants, thereby benefiting the restaurateurs and the industry in the following ways...." You would then proceed to document the contributions that you probably would have liked to have been able to say were benefits from your study alone, but now can better justify stating might-be benefits if all the parallel studies suggested are undertaken (and if all of them conclude in the same way your study has concluded). Here, too, you can use a disclaimer to generalize from your study.

Writing the "Recommendations for Further Study" Section

As work on Chapter Two of the thesis developed, you probably found an uneven mixture of previous research that had been done in the field. Some aspects of the topic may have been overresearched; other aspects may have been underresearched. In fact, you may find that no previous research has been done for several major aspects of your thesis research question. As you go on with the thesis study, you may find that little or no research has been conducted in significant areas relating to some of the study outcomes and conclusions. All of these underresearched or nonresearched areas present opportunities for those interested in pursuing further hospitality industry research. To bring attention to the need for further research, state what the needs are, possibly ranking the research needs, and indicate statistical and other data that may support your claim that additional research needs to be completed in this topic area.

Writing the "Contributions of the Study" Section

The "Contributions of the Study" section of the thesis is intended to identify how the study and the information developed from the study can contribute to the industry. If you have selected a topic that will provide new information needed within a specific segment of the industry or within the industry as a whole, and if you have considered from the outset techniques or approaches to use in disseminating this new information, this section should be easy to write. Students often select topics that fail to meet these criteria, however. As noted, unless the study can contribute to the industry, it should not be done. Therefore, the writing of this section is intended to serve the purpose of showing specific recommended applications of the new knowledge derived from the study.

The recommendations should be clear and precise. Most important, they should be realistic. To suggest that hotel chains, restaurant chains, or "all domestic" airlines will somehow obtain the results of the data and will change their operating procedures accordingly is unrealistic. Instead, you should identify how the results can be applied to one or more specific segments of the industry (for example, several hotels, one or two air carrier training departments, or a small chain of restaurants).

Recommend realistic and practical ways of disseminating the information. Some of the best ways of disseminating the information include making presentations at professional conferences, writing professional journal articles, and sending a synopsis of study results to interested industry individuals (following up with either a letter or a phone call). Any one of these techniques may suffice to get the new information derived from the study reviewed and considered. An even better alternative is a combination of two or all three of these approaches.

Writing the Chapter Five Conclusion

The Chapter Five conclusion is, in essence, a five-chapter package. This conclusion is more than just a summary of Chapter Five. You must summarize the high points of Chapter Five, and you must bring together a conclusion or a summary of the entire thesis.

Start this summary with one or two paragraphs that identify the main points in chapter five. These will be the overall conclusions and the major editorial points relating to the conclusions of the study. In the same one or two paragraphs or in a separate paragraph, you should next summarize the contributions of the study. Finally, in a one- or two-paragraph conclusion to the study, you should provide an overview of the entire study. This can be done by boiling down the major points identified in each of the five chapters into two or three sentences per chapter, reviewing the sentences, and inserting transition words or sentences.

Summary

Chapter Five consists of your interpretation of the results of the research, the conclusion of the study, recommendations for further study, and the contributions of the study.

The introduction is a transition between Chapter Four and Chapter Five, including a summary or overview of the global interpretations based on the factual results found in Chapter Four.

The bulk of Chapter Five is made up of interpretations derived from the statistical outcomes generated in Chapter Four. The development of these interpretations follows the same flow as that found in Chapter Four. Because the two chapters are so closely interrelated you can write most or all of the interpretations for Chapter Five while you are working on Chapter Four. They are set aside until Chapter Five is written.

The flow starts with the development of the interpretation of data at the lowest level—with the research items that back up a specific subproblem. This is the same set of research instrument items (questions) backing up the same subproblem with which Chapter Four started. As with Chapter Four, move from one subproblem to the next, from one problem to the next, from one hypothesis to the next, and finally to the research question, in each case providing interpretations based on the statistical data that was developed in Chapter Four.

Conclude the interpretations with global interpretations limited to the parameters of the study itself. You may want to generalize beyond the parameters of your study, but you must stay within the tenets of quality research. This is handled by writing disclaimers and then suggesting generalizations in the following sections.

Next, you develop the "Recommendations for Further Study" and "Contributions of the Study" sections. The global interpretations usually raise further study needs and relate closely to contributions. Before writing the "Contributions of the Study" section, go back to the "Importance of the Study" section of Chapter One. The contributions and the importance should relate closely, although as the thesis was developed, additional contributions were probably identified. After recognizing the potential contributions of the study, identify how information related to the study will be disseminated to the industry.

The final part of Chapter Five is the conclusion. As with many of the other chapter conclusions, this is a two-part conclusion. The first part is a summary of Chapter Five; the second part is an overall conclusion of the entire thesis.

Discussion Questions

These questions may be discussed by two or more students outside of class, or they may be discussed during class for a more wide-ranging discussion.

1. Why is Chapter Five the chapter that most student researchers enjoy writing the most?

2. The final part of Chapter Five is a one- or two-paragraph conclusion to the study. How is this prepared?

3. What is the final step in the interpretation of the data?

4. What are some good ways of disseminating information about your thesis and its potential contributions to the industry?

5. How is Chapter Five started?

6. What criteria should be met by each of the recommended applications of information derived from the study?

7. At least half of the introduction to Chapter Five is usually devoted to what?

8. The global interpretation of the results of the overall study are listed numerically and then treated one by one. What does this treatment involve?

9. Why should you prepare the conclusion and the interpretation sections of much of Chapter Five while you are working on Chapter Four?

10. Why is it that the process followed in interpreting the conclusions regarding the problem and the research question is not completed while Chapter Four is being developed?

Role Play Exercises

Two students may participate in these role play exercises either outside of class or as in-class exercises. One plays the role of the first student and the other plays the role of the second student. Read the scripts and then pick up the conversations in your own words.

1. **FIRST STUDENT:** This chapter suggests that many of the interpretations of data are easier to write if they are prepared at the same time that work on Chapter Four is undertaken. Since Chapter Four simply presents the statistical results and doesn't allow for interpretations, this recommendation to prepare the Chapter Five sections at the same time doesn't make sense to me.

    SECOND STUDENT: It may not make sense, but there is some logic in the recommendation. As with everything else, however, there are both advantages and disadvantages to preparing the Chapter Five interpretations while working on Chapter Four. Let me explain why many people do prepare the interpretations while writing Chapter Four—and then I'll explain the pros and cons of that process. Let's start by considering the fact that in writing Chapter Four you. . . .

    ### Continue on Your Own

2. **FIRST STUDENT:** Why should I have to recommend applications of the knowledge and information derived from my study in the "Contributions of the Study" section? Isn't it enough that I simply tell the reader how my study could theoretically contribute to the industry?

    SECOND STUDENT: That word, "theoretical," is the key. If you did not move from the theoretical contribution to applications of new knowledge and techniques for disseminating that knowledge, the presumed contributions might remain presumed or theoretical only. That is of limited value to the hospitality industry.

    FIRST STUDENT: That is arguable, but I understand the point. Okay, how can I identify those people in the industry who might use the results of my study and consider it a practical contribution? Once I identify the right people, what do I realistically do to get them to pay any attention to it or to do anything with the results?

    SECOND STUDENT: Those are the right questions to be asking in order to prepare the applications portion of the "Contributions of the Study" section of Chapter Five. Let's take the questions one by one starting with. . . .

    ### Continue on Your Own

3. **FIRST STUDENT:** I'm having a serious problem in putting together the pieces of Chapter Five. Each section I have written just doesn't seem to fit with any of the other sections; I'm not even sure that what I have put together is complete.

SECOND STUDENT: As with every other chapter in the thesis, there is a specific flow that is recommended. Usually if you follow this flow and put in some good transition sentences, you will have at least a good first draft.

FIRST STUDENT: I think I understand the sequencing and I have tried to follow it, but the end result still just does not seem to fit.

SECOND STUDENT: It sounds like you do have a problem. Let me review with you the sequencing so that we both make sure we agree on the flow of information and sections in Chapter Five. Then tell or show me what you have done. Together we should be able to find the problem and get it worked out. First, let me explain the sequencing. It starts with . . .

Continue on Your Own

12.1. Pre-Chapter One Pages

Review the first drafts of pre-Chapter One pages that you prepared as the first exercise in Chapter 3 of this book (Exercise 3.1). Also review the evaluation of these pages by your professor. Next, go over all five chapters of your thesis, noting the page numbers and titles of each section, chart, graph, figure, and table.

Prepare the same pre-Chapter One pages, but this time prepare them in the same way as you plan to turn them in with your final thesis. A few changes may be made later as you add table of contents information relating to the appendixes to the study. However, most of the documents you are preparing now can be considered final documents for your thesis.

The preliminary pages that you will need to prepare for this assignment include the outside thesis cover title page, the inside title page, the table of contents, a table of charts, a table of graphs, a table of figures, and a table of tables. Be sure to type your name at the top of each of the copies of the pages that you plan to hand in for this assignment. The originals will go into your completed thesis. These originals should be retained by you and should *not* have your name typed on them.

To the copies of your completed preliminary pages, attach an Instructor Comment Sheet. Make sure the Instructor Comment Sheet has the Assignment section filled in and that it has your name on it. Place the copies of the preliminary pages and the Instructor Comment Sheet into an 8.5" × 11" manila envelope with a clasp flap with your name typed on the front of the envelope. If your instructor requests it, include a blank, top-quality audiotape (30 minutes) with your name printed on it, so that your professor may give you feedback.

12.2. The "Contributions of the Study" Section and the "Recommendations for Further" Study Section

Review the portions of this chapter that relate to the writing of the "Contributions of the Study" and the "Recommendations for Further Study" sections. Based on this information and your own research, prepare the "Contributions of the Study" section and the "Recommendations for Further Study" section of Chapter Five of your thesis. Be sure to type your name at the top of each page.

To your completed sections, attach an Instructor Comment Sheet. Make sure the Instructor Comment Sheet has the Assignment section filled in and that it has your name on it. Place the two completed sections and the Instructor Comment Sheet into an 8.5" × 11" manila envelope with a clasp flap with your name typed on the front of the envelope. If your instructor requests it, include a blank, top-quality audiotape (30 minutes long) with your name printed on it, so that your professor may give you feedback.

12.3. Chapter Five

Review this chapter. Based on the information in this chapter and your own research, prepare Chapter Five of your thesis. Be sure to type your name at the top of each page.

Unless you provide justification for not including one of them, the following sections should be included: (1) an introduction to the chapter; (2) the findings (a detailed description of the statistical results as stated in Chapter Four); (3) the interpretation of the data (interpretations from the findings in the same order as the findings are reported in Chapter Four); (4) the interpretation of conclusions for each hypothesis; (5) the interpretation of conclusions for the problem and for the research question; (6) the contributions of the study; (7) recommendations for further study; and (8) the chapter and the thesis conclusion. Make certain that there is a smooth transition from one section to the next throughout the chapter.

To your completed chapter, attach an Instructor Comment Sheet. Make sure the Instructor Comment Sheet has the Assignment section filled in and that it has your name on it. Place Chapter Five and the Instructor Comment sheet into an 8.5" × 11" manila envelope with a clasp flap with your name typed on the envelope. If your instructor requests it, include a blank, top-quality audiotape (30 minutes long) with your name printed on it, so that your professor may give you feedback.

CHAPTER THIRTEEN

Post-Study Tasks

U*pon completion of this chapter, you will be able to:*

1. Write a synopsis of your thesis.

2. List all components of the completed thesis in the order in which they are to be bound prior to turning the thesis in for a grade.

3. Prepare a cover letter tailored to your thesis synopsis.

4. Identify publications (and the appropriate editors of those publications) for the potential publication of your thesis, synopsis, or an article based on your thesis.

Introduction

The thesis is now essentially completed, and most student researchers are doubly happy. They are pleased that the work of writing the thesis has essentially been completed, and they are usually proud of the thesis that they have written. They have every reason to be proud. Only a small percentage of the population ever authors a formal study of this depth.

However, the work is not yet complete. There are still several post-study tasks that need to be undertaken. This chapter discusses those tasks. The post-study tasks include the required jobs of preparing the addenda to the thesis, packaging the original research study (including the addenda), writing the research study synopsis, writing thank-you letters, and mailing the synopsis and thank-you letters to those who have contributed to the study. These four tasks are required by most academicians who oversee the writing of theses. In addition, the optional task of getting the thesis published is a desirable option that is undertaken by many thesis writers.

The Addenda

Some academicians require students to include as their initial addendum (called an appendix) the original responses to the questionnaire. These will be titled "Original

Questionnaire Responses"; the originals will be bound into the first or "master" copy of the thesis, and photocopies are bound into additional copies. The requirement to include original responses is made so that the professor can make certain that basic analysis work completed in Chapter Four was completed accurately. Some checks for accuracy are impossible to complete without the availability of the raw data. Professors requiring this data maintain that confidentiality of data is not violated, because the thesis with the original questionnaire responses included is not circulated and is read by only the student who authored it and the professor who guided the student's research effort.

Many professors also require the following addenda: (1) a copy of the form cover letter that accompanied the questionnaire when it was mailed to potential respondents; (2) a copy of the mailing list of those to whom the questionnaire was mailed; (3) a blank copy of the original questionnaire; (4) a copy of the synopsis that was sent to questionnaire respondents; and (5) a copy of the cover letter sent with the synopsis to questionnaire respondents. A few academicians require all five of these addenda, but most require only a few, and some require none of them. Check with your professor to determine which documents are required as addenda and which are not.

In addition to required addenda, you may want to include additional addenda. Frequently, one or more of the respondents to the questionnaire will send back material with the completed questionnaire. In some cases this material is appropriate to include as an addendum; in other cases it is not. Use your own judgment in making this determination. If there is a question about whether or not material should be included as an addendum, check with your professor.

In addition to material that may be sent with a completed questionnaire by a respondent, you may want to include additional data. Such items may include the following: brochures; hotel, airline, meeting, restaurant, or other management development programs; industry salary surveys; questionnaire tabulations; dissertation abstracts; copies of articles taken from single or multiple trade or other sources (with permission); printed excerpts; personality test copies (for example, the Myers Briggs test); samples of hiring criteria developed and used by sample companies in the hospitality industry; extended bibliographies; telephone survey results; sample telemarketing scripts; letters received from industry executives; industry applicant information sheets; sample interview questions; interview screening forms; and interview information profiles. Any document or collection of documents that you and your professor feel are appropriate may be included. Each addendum is called an appendix and is labeled as such, ordered and numbered sequentially.

Make certain that all appendixes are appropriately titled. Identify each appendix sequentially by number or letter; a brief title should appear on the appendix cover sheet. All appendixes are placed after Chapter Five and the Chapter Five footnotes and bibliography. They are placed in the order of their appearance on the table of contents.

Packaging the Original Research Study

Many educational institutions have specific criteria as to how to package theses and the number of copies that are required. If these are documented, request a copy of the guidelines and follow them exactly. If they are not spelled out in writing, use the following recommendations as a guide, and check with your professor to determine whether or not the policies of your institution and the program in which you are enrolled agree with them. If they do not, your institution's procedures and policies apply and should be followed. Review Figure 13.1 for a visual display of the packaging order.

The number of copies required may vary, from only the original, to the original plus one copy, to the original plus as many as five copies. Most colleges and universities will

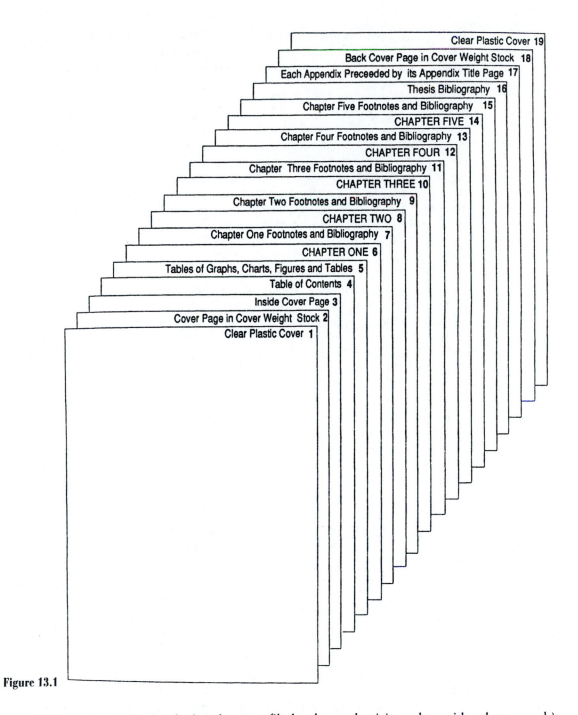

Clear Plastic Cover 19
Back Cover Page in Cover Weight Stock 18
Each Appendix Preceeded by its Appendix Title Page 17
Thesis Bibliography 16
Chapter Five Footnotes and Bibliography 15
CHAPTER FIVE 14
Chapter Four Footnotes and Bibliography 13
CHAPTER FOUR 12
Chapter Three Footnotes and Bibliography 11
CHAPTER THREE 10
Chapter Two Footnotes and Bibliography 9
CHAPTER TWO 8
Chapter One Footnotes and Bibliography 7
CHAPTER ONE 6
Tables of Graphs, Charts, Figures and Tables 5
Table of Contents 4
Inside Cover Page 3
Cover Page in Cover Weight Stock 2
Clear Plastic Cover 1

Figure 13.1

require an original (which is kept on file by the academician who guides the research) and a copy (which is available for the student to pick up and retain once it has been graded). The professor usually comments directly onto the student's copy of the thesis, or the comments can be made on an audiotape (provided by the student). In a few cases, the comments are made directly on both the student's copy and on the original (which is retained by the professor).

The form of binding of the thesis may be left up to you, or a particular type may be required. Uniform bindings that are frequently used include three-ring binding, velobinding, bookbinding, and spiral binding. Determine the preference of the academic program or your professor. Velobinding and spiral binding are increasingly popular because they are inexpensive and almost any copy facility is equipped to do them, usually while you wait.

The size of the final thesis document should also be considered. Most academic institutions require that inside paper size be no more than 8.5" × 11" and that the covers be either the same size or only slightly larger (usually in a standard cover size).

The front and back covers are usually heavier than regular copy paper, and are usually available in standard cover-page weight. For velobinding and spiral binding, a clear plastic cover, which is placed on top of the cover-weight paper stock (on which the thesis title and sometimes other information is printed), is available in most copy shops. It is inexpensive and will protect the thesis from wear and tear. Some academic departments and academicians mandate that a clear plastic outside cover be used, some mandate that clear plastic covers *not* be used, and some leave the use of clear plastic covers to your discretion.

The order in which documents are bound into each copy of the thesis is as follows: (1) clear plastic cover; (2) cover page in cover-weight stock; (3) inside cover page; (4) table of contents; (5) tables of graphs, charts, figures, and tables; (6) Chapter One; (7) Chapter One footnotes and bibliography; (8) Chapter Two; (9) Chapter Two footnotes and bibliography; (10) Chapter Three; (11) Chapter Three footnotes and bibliography; (12) Chapter Four; (13) Chapter Four footnotes and bibliography; (14) Chapter Five; (15) Chapter Five footnotes and bibliography; (16) thesis bibliography; (17) the appendixes, each preceded by an appendix title page; (18) back page in cover-weight stock; and (19) clear plastic cover. Although this order may vary slightly from one department or institution to another (check with your professor), the order listed is standard and is followed by most academic institutions.

The front cover page and the back page in cover-weight stock may be of a standard color. Your institution may have written requirements specifying the color. Some have a preprinted cover page that can be obtained from a printer used by the department, from the department secretary, or your instructor. There is usually a cost for this, but you have the advantage of having a cover supplied to you. When such a standard cover is used, you need only insert it into a typewriter, word processor, or computer and enter the title of the thesis and your name (in some cases, your name will not appear on the outside cover, but will appear only on the inside cover; check this with your professor).

Once the original and all copies of the thesis have been bound, they should be inserted into a large manila envelope. Make certain that the envelope has a metal clasp or a tie bind so that the envelope will not have to be sealed permanently. Affix a label to the outside of the envelope. Type the following information on the label: (1) (number of) copies of final bound thesis; (2) your name; (3) your social security number; (4) your address; and (5) your work (if appropriate) and home phone numbers. All copies of the thesis should be turned in to your professor in one envelope, so that the professor will not have several loose copies of the thesis.

Many academicians prefer to have all thesis copies handed in to the department secretary or placed in the professor's box in the departmental office. This keeps the professor from having to carry a large number of theses from the classroom to the office. Check with your professor to determine when and how the thesis copies should be turned in.

Note that when the grading of the thesis will be done on audiotape, it is customary to require the inclusion of a blank audiotape with your name printed on the tape label and affixed to the blank tape. The tape is placed in the envelope with the thesis. Check with your professor to determine whether or not this requirement will apply.

Some professors require students to include a self-addressed, stamped envelope, which is used to send you your copy of the graded thesis. This allows your copy of the thesis to be returned to you in a timely manner. If an audiotape is required, make sure that the self-addressed, stamped envelope is large enough to hold the thesis and the audio tape. Take the envelope to the post office for weighing with a copy of the thesis and a blank tape (including the tape's plastic cover box). This will ensure that sufficient postage is affixed to the return envelope.

Writing the Research Study Synopsis

The synopsis is a summary or overview of the study, with the concentration being placed on the outcomes. It serves several purposes, but the major use of the synopsis is to provide results to those who contributed to the thesis. It is considered polite and appropriate to send the results of the study to those who contributed to the study by completing questionnaires. In addition to those who responded to questionnaires, synopses are often sent to other contributors, such as those who may have responded to a telephone survey or who may have contributed written material for the study.

Synopses also are used if you wish to publish your thesis or an article based on your thesis. The synopsis is submitted to editors and publishers with an appropriate cover letter.

Finally, the synopsis can be used if you wish to make a presentation to a professional organization. The synopsis provides the committee charged with selecting speakers with an understanding of the basic content of your thesis. This helps the committee select topics and speakers.

The synopsis should be short. Most synopses are no more than one page in length. They are usually single-spaced and have a brief heading at the top: "Synopsis of (title of topic)." This is followed by your name on the next line. After skipping two spaces, the synopsis starts with an introduction. The body of the synopsis comes next, and the conclusion is the last part of the synopsis.

In writing the synopsis, most people find that writing the body first, the introduction second, and the conclusion last works best. In preparing the body of the synopsis, a common way to start is to review each chapter, writing one or two sentences summarizing each. Chapters Four and Five deal with the results; each result should be set out very clearly. This need not identify that the result is a proof for or against the hypothesis or that the conclusion being drawn relates to a particular subproblem or problem number, but it is common to identify the research question and the result of the research question and to identify the research problems and the conclusions relating to them.

After this initial summary of chapters and discussion of results has been set out, you may find that more than a single page of paper has been used. The next step is to condense the results and the summary, smoothing out the transitions from one idea to the next and eliminating references to problems, subproblems, and any possible overuse of such terms as "research question." This review and condensation of material should continue until not more than two-thirds of a single page of paper is used.

Next, the introduction is written. In order to write it, the body of the thesis is reviewed and a few (usually not more than three or four) sentences are written to introduce the body.

The conclusion is written in much the same way. Again, the body of the material is reviewed and a three- or four-sentence conclusion is written.

In writing the synopsis, do not include superfluous comments or editorialism that would more appropriately fit into the cover letter. Remember that the synopsis is written to serve several purposes, one of which is to provide the high points of the study results and an overview of the study for contributors, potential publishers, and speaker-selection committees. Editorial comments to contributors are more appropriately placed in the cover letter, rather than the synopsis itself.

Thank-You Letters and Synopsis Distribution

Once the synopsis has been completed, copies should be reproduced in sufficient number that at least one copy can go to each person who contributed to the study. It should be mailed with an appropriate cover letter.

The cover letter should include a brief reminder to the recipient about the study. Because the recipient may have completed the questionnaire several months before, the recipient may have forgotten about the study. Briefly remind the recipient that he or she has contributed to the study and thank the recipient for this contribution.

Next, the cover letter should state that the study has been completed and that a synopsis of the study, including an overview of the major outcomes, is attached. If your college or university allows interested parties to review completed theses, indicate this, and identify what arrangements a person would need to make to peruse the full study. If, however, your college or university does not allow a perusal of completed studies by members of the public, or if it does not have a system set up for such a review, it is better not to state this fact. Ignore the matter altogether, completing the letter with a recognition that the synopsis is attached and finishing with a brief one- or two-sentence paragraph again thanking the recipient for contributing to it.

Some educators require that all thank-you letters and synopses be mailed from the college, and some colleges and universities underwrite the cost of this mailing. Check with your professor to determine what the policy of your institution is before mailing the synopses and cover letters.

Publishing and Otherwise Using the Thesis

As noted earlier, it is recommended that using the thesis to make a contribution to the industry be considered. This is most commonly done through publishing the study itself, the synopsis, or an article based on the study. Presentations to industry associations or other interested groups presents another opportunity for distributing the information determined as a result of the study.

In publishing, the first step is to identify a publication that would be appropriate for the thesis or, more commonly, for an article based on the outcomes of the thesis. Consider the resources identified and referenced in Chapter Two of the thesis. Generally, the same publications that are drawn on for Chapter Two are the publications that would most likely be interested in publishing the thesis, the synopsis, or an article based on the thesis outcomes. It is always better to identify two or three potential publications rather than only one. If you are having difficulty in identifying an appropriate publication, ask your professor. The professor should be able to provide information about publications that may be more obscure, but might also be more appropriate for and more interested in your thesis.

Once a publication has been identified, find the name of the publisher or editor and submit your thesis, synopsis, and/or article concept with an appropriate cover letter. If you have not received a response within four weeks, call the publication. Be prepared to discuss the potential for publication during this phone call. It is always wise when making such phone calls to have a copy of the thesis, synopsis, and article concept in front of you.

Making a verbal presentation based on the outcomes of your thesis is approached in much the same way. The initial step is to determine what organization, association, club, or other group would have a special interest in the subject on which your thesis was written. Contact the president, meeting planner, or convention chairperson; send a cover letter indicating your interest in making a presentation based on the outcomes of your thesis. Include a copy of the synopsis or thesis (usually the synopsis is preferred at this point). As with publishing, if you do not hear back within four weeks, follow up with a phone call.

A published article or a presentation based on your thesis present opportunities for additional exposure within the industry. Publication credits enhance your résumé. Both verbal and written presentations provide additional marketability in terms of getting a first (or a better) job in the hospitality industry.

Summary

Although the thesis is essentially finished with the completion of the fifth chapter, there are several post-study tasks that need to be accomplished. Addenda in the form of appendixes need to be prepared, and a synopsis needs to be written to be sent to those who contributed to the study. The synopsis is accompanied by an appropriate cover letter. The entire research study package needs to be put together and turned in for a grade.

Consideration needs to be given to publishing the thesis, the synopsis, or an article based on the study. Industry presentations based on the outcomes of the thesis present another way of distributing information developed through the thesis to those in the industry who are interested in receiving this information.

This chapter identifies the information needed to accomplish these tasks. It also suggests processes for completing the major post-study tasks associated with writing a thesis.

Discussion Questions

These questions may be discussed by two or more students outside of class, or they may be discussed during class for a more wide-ranging discussion.

1. What four post-study tasks are usually required by most academicians who oversee the writing of theses?

2. In preparing to make a presentation based on the outcomes of your thesis, what initial step should you take?

3. What is the first addendum to the thesis that is required by many academicians who direct thesis research?

4. What additional addenda (as many as five) do a few academicians who direct theses require?

5. After sending out a letter, synopsis, thesis, or article concept to a publisher or editor to determine potential interest in publishing the thesis, synopsis, or article, approximately how long should you wait before placing a follow-up call to the editor or publisher?

6. In addition to a number or letter code for the appendix, what else should appear on the appendix cover sheet?

7. Why should the thank-you letter, which is mailed with the synopsis, include a brief reminder to the recipient about the study?

8. What four types of thesis binding were listed in this chapter?

9. In writing the synopsis, should you start with the introduction, the body, or the conclusion?

10. What is the usual order for binding documents into each copy of the thesis?

Role Play Exercises

Two students may participate in these role play exercises either outside of class or as in-class exercises. One plays the role of the first student and the other plays the role of the second student. Read the scripts and then pick up the conversations in your own words.

1. FIRST STUDENT: I think the idea of publishing my thesis or an article based on my thesis or making a speech about it is a great idea. I think I want to try it. But even after reading about it and listening to our professor talk about it, I still don't feel like I know where to begin. An article based on your thesis was published. What do you suggest?

    SECOND STUDENT: Start by following the guidelines suggested in the chapter. You first need to...

Continue on Your Own

2. FIRST STUDENT: I think I've got everything together ready to bind my thesis. But I still don't really understand exactly what goes where or in what order.

    SECOND STUDENT: Let's look at all the pieces you have gotten together. Do you have them here?

    FIRST STUDENT: I've made a list of them. Tell me the sequence and I'll simply number the parts as we go through them. Then I can go back and put them in the sequenced order, ready for binding.

    SECOND STUDENT: That seems like a good approach. The first component of the final bound thesis on the very top is...

Continue On Your Own

3. FIRST STUDENT: I have been thinking about the packaging necessary for everything that is handed in for a grade. I know I need to have the final bound thesis in an envelope. What else is needed? What is the best kind of envelope to get which will hold everything I need to put in it? I don't want it to cost me a fortune.

    SECOND STUDENT: The items that need to go into the envelope depend partially on what you want to get back and when you want to get them back. The envelope itself should obviously be a strong one. But there are some other considerations as well. Let me first explain what you should look for in an envelope and then I will tell you in detail what your options are in terms of all the things you will need to put into the envelope. In considering the envelope, first of all you need to make sure that it is...

Continue On Your Own

13.1. Completed Cover Letter and Synopsis Ready to Mail

Prepare the mailing of your synopses and cover letters to all persons who sent you back a fully or partially completed research instrument questionnaire. Also prepare envelopes for others who may have contributed in some other way to your thesis study. Do not seal the envelopes. Place them in envelope boxes or boxes of a similar size ready to mail, but not sealed. Set up an appointment with your professor so that your mailing can be checked before the envelopes are sealed and you deliver the mailing to the post office.

Before meeting with your professor to check this assignment, review the information in this chapter (and from your research) relating to the preparation of synopsis mailings. Prepare an Instructor Comment Sheet and bring it with you to the meeting with your professor. Make sure the Instructor Comment Sheet has the Assignment section filled in and that it has your name on it. When you give the professor your boxes of unsealed envelopes to check, also give him or her your Instructor Comment Sheet in an 8.5" × 11" manila envelope with a clasp flap with your name typed on the front of the envelope. (You do not need to include an audiotape; your professor will be able to tell you about any problems in person.)

13.2. Addenda

Review this chapter. Based on the information in this chapter and your own research, prepare one set of the addenda for your thesis.

Unless you provide justification for not including one of them, the following addenda should be included: (1) copies of the "Original Questionnaire Responses" as addendum number one; (2) a copy of the cover letter that accompanied the questionnaire when it was mailed to potential respondents; (3) a copy of the mailing list; (4) a blank copy of the original questionnaire; (5) a copy of the synopsis that was sent to questionnaire respondents; and (6) a copy of the cover letter sent with the synopsis to questionnaire respondents. In addition, include any other addenda that you (and your professor) feel should be included. Make sure that you include a title page for each addendum to be included in your thesis.

To your completed addenda (and title pages), attach an Instructor Comment Sheet. Make sure the Instructor Comment Sheet has the Assignment section filled in and that it has your name on it. Place the addenda (and title pages) and the Instructor Comment Sheet into an 8.5" × 11" manila envelope with a clasp flap with your name typed on the envelope. Include a blank, top-quality audiotape (30 minutes long) with your name printed on it, so that your professor may give you feedback.

13.3. Packaged Original Research Study

Review this chapter. Based on the information in this chapter and your research, prepare a minimum of one original and one copy of your entire bound thesis to be provided to your professor for a grade. Check with your professor to determine the exact number of copies that should be prepared.

Unless you provide justification for not including one of them, the following components should be included: (1) a clear plastic cover; (2) a cover page in cover-weight stock; (3) an inside cover page; (4) the table of contents; (5) tables of graphs, charts, figures, and tables; (6) Chapter One; (7) Chapter One footnotes and bibliography; (8) Chapter Two; (9) Chapter Two footnotes and bibliography; (10) Chapter Three; (11) Chapter Three footnotes and bibliography; (12) Chapter Four; (13) Chapter Four footnotes and bibliography; (14) Chapter Five; (15) Chapter Five footnotes and bibliography; (16) the thesis bibliography; (17) the appendixes, each preceded by an appropriate appendix title page; (18) a back page in cover-weight stock; and (19) a clear plastic back cover for the thesis. In addition, include any other material that you and your professor feel should be included. Make sure all copies are bound according to the policies and procedures established by your academic institution or your professor.

To your completed thesis, attach an Instructor Comment Sheet. Make sure the Instructor Comment Sheet has the Assignment section filled in and that it has your name on it. Place the original and all required copies of your thesis and the Instructor Comment Sheet into a large manila envelope with a metal clasp or a tie bind, so that the envelope will not have to be sealed permanently. Type the following as the first line on a label to be affixed to the outside of the envelope: "(number of copies) copies of final bound thesis." The second line on the label should be your name. The third line on the label should be your social security number. Additional lines should show your address and your work (if appropriate) and home phone numbers. Affix the label to the outside of the envelope in a clearly readable position. If your instructor requests it, include a blank, top-quality audiotape (30 minutes long) with your name printed on it, so that your professor may give you feedback. Check with your professor to determine where and how this package is to be turned in.

Index

Instructor Comment Sheet

Assignment: _____

Instructor's Comments: _____

_____

_____

_____

Points have been deducted from the score indicated below for the following reasons:

_____ days late @ _____ points per day = _____points

Assignment not typed @ _____ points _____points

English language error @ _____ points each _____points

Other _____ _____points

POINTS

01	02	03	04	05
06	07	08	09	10
11	12	13	14	15
16	17	18	19	20
21	22	23	24	25
26	27	28	29	30

Student Name: _____

Instructor Comment Sheet

Assignment: _____

Instructor's Comments: _____

_____

_____

_____

Points have been deducted from the score indicated below for the following reasons:

_____ days late @   points per day = _____points

Assignment not typed @   points   _____points

English language error @   points each   _____points

Other _____   _____points

POINTS

01	02	03	04	05
06	07	08	09	10
11	12	13	14	15
16	17	18	19	20
21	22	23	24	25
26	27	28	29	30

Instructor Comment Sheet

Assignment: _____

Instructor's Comments: _____

_____

_____

_____

Points have been deducted from the score indicated below for the following reasons:

_____ days late @   points per day = _____points

Assignment not typed @   points   _____points

English language error @   points each   _____points

Other _____   _____points

POINTS

01	02	03	04	05
06	07	08	09	10
11	12	13	14	15
16	17	18	19	20
21	22	23	24	25
26	27	28	29	30

Student Name: _____

Instructor Comment Sheet

Assignment: _____

Instructor's Comments: _____

_____

_____

_____

Points have been deducted from the score indicated below for the following reasons:

_____ days late @ _____ points per day = _____points

Assignment not typed @ _____ points _____points

English language error @ _____ points each _____points

Other _____ _____points

POINTS

01	02	03	04	05
06	07	08	09	10
11	12	13	14	15
16	17	18	19	20
21	22	23	24	25
26	27	28	29	30

Instructor Comment Sheet

Assignment: _____

Instructor's Comments: _____

_____

_____

_____

Points have been deducted from the score indicated below for the following reasons:

____ days late @   points per day = _____ points

Assignment not typed @   points   _____ points

English language error @   points each   _____ points

Other _____   _____ points

POINTS

01	02	03	04	05
06	07	08	09	10
11	12	13	14	15
16	17	18	19	20
21	22	23	24	25
26	27	28	29	30

Instructor Comment Sheet

Assignment: _____

Instructor's Comments: _____

_____

_____

_____

Points have been deducted from the score indicated below for the following reasons:

____ days late @   points per day = _____points

Assignment not typed @   points   _____points

English language error @   points each   _____points

Other _____   _____points

POINTS

01	02	03	04	05
06	07	08	09	10
11	12	13	14	15
16	17	18	19	20
21	22	23	24	25
26	27	28	29	30

Instructor Comment Sheet

Assignment: _____

Instructor's Comments: _____

_____

_____

_____

Points have been deducted from the score indicated below for the following reasons:

_____ days late @ _____ points per day = _____points

Assignment not typed @ _____ points _____points

English language error @ _____ points each _____points

Other _____ _____points

POINTS

01	02	03	04	05
06	07	08	09	10
11	12	13	14	15
16	17	18	19	20
21	22	23	24	25
26	27	28	29	30